I0090219

Oddities in English

For Anyone Wanting To Speak English
Fluently But Perplexed By All Of The
Oddities
In English Grammar and Pronunciation

Jesús Núñez Romay

blue ocean press
tokyo

Published by:

blue ocean press, an Imprint of Aoishima Research Institute (ARI)
#807-36 Lions Plaza Ebisu
3-25-3 Higashi, Shibuya-ku
Tokyo, Japan 150-0011

mail@aoishima-research.com
URL: http://www.aoishima-research.com

Author:Jesús Núñez Romay, Profesor Auxiliar, CNIC
Edición: Lic. Esteban Pérez Fernández
Composición: Yamira Puig Fernández
Corrección: Prof. Jesús A. Núñez Romay
Lic. Esteban Pérez Fernández
Emplane y realización: Lic. Esteban Pérez Fernández
Diseño de cubierta: Ramón Jiménez Sánchez
Sobre la presente edición: Editorial CENIC Enero de 1997.

ISBN: 978-4-902837-05-6

Table of Contents

In loving memory of my parents.

To my beloved son, Edgar.

Introduccion (Introduction)

El presente trabajo es el fruto de más de tres lustros de ejercicio docente en la Enseñanza Superior y está dirigido a todos aquellos especialistas del idioma inglés, o estudiantes no filólogos que hayan buscado en más de una ocasión una explicación a ciertas irregularidades de la lengua de Shakespeare sin encontrar en texto alguno, solución a sus interrogantes.

El libro está dividido en varios rubros que han sido puntos álgidos en el desarrollo del trabajo docente frente al alumno. Las fuentes bibliográficas principales han sido los documentos sociales utilizados en esa tarea, así como de investigación lingüística durante varios años.

En principio, el texto ha sido estructurado como material de apoyo a los Cursos de Idioma Inglés, que se imparten en el Centro Nacional de Investigaciones Científicas, pero pudiera servir como medio de consulta o ampliación de conocimientos para los estudiosos del idioma.

Cada material ha sido revisado y consultado convenientemente con especialistas de la docencia y de la traducción.

Para concluir, quisiera expresar mi más profundo reconocimiento a cuantos, de una manera u otra, contribuyeron a la elaboración de este material. Entre ellos, al Profesor Auxiliar Ricardo J. Cepero Ferrer, del Departamento de Inglés-Francés del Instituto Superior Pedagógico "Enrique Jos Varona", por despertar en mí la inquietud sobre varios de estos temas. A la Profesora Titular Marjorie Moore Reynolds del Instituto Superior de Ciencias Médicas "Victoria de Girón", por sus consejos y cooperación en los contenidos presentados.

A la Licenciada Mary Todd Haessler, especialista en traducción del E.S.T.I., por su ayuda sistemática a través de los últimos años de mi carrera profesional, y la revisión de cada acápite.

La Profesora Asistente Joan Cutting, del Instituto Superior de Ciencias Médicas de La Habana "Victoria de Girón", y a

Lila Haynes, de Radio Habana Cuba, por la asesoría de ambas en el capítulo que tiene en cuenta la norma Británica.

Al Profesor Asistente Carlos Franco Bello, de la Facultad de Medicina "Miguel Enríquez", por su colaboración en varios de estos aspectos.

Asimismo, deseo hacer patente mi agradecimiento por el trabajo editorial y de composición a mis alumnos Licenciado Esteban Pérez Fernández, del Centro Nacional de Investigaciones Científicas y la compañera Yamira Puig Fernández del Centro Nacional de Biopreparados respectivamente.

Profesor Jesús A. Núñez Romay.

Chapter 1
Special Difficulties and
Common Errors in English

The following groups of words are usually mistaken among students who take English as a second language. We have not included, of course, all the items which could lead to misunderstanding and mistakes in conversation, because this would be material for a book by far. Nevertheless, we do wish to include some of the most commonly mistaken expressions and words that our students fall prey of.

Understanding and understandable
Ex. She's a very understanding person.
      (She's able to understand others)
   The exercise is not very understandable to us.
      (Easy to be understood)

Couple and pair
Ex. I bought a couple of links.
      (Two things that are united)
   She has a pair of gloves.
      (Things that must be taken together to be useful)

Dairy and diary
Ex. I bought an ice cream at the dairy.
      (place for milk products)
   We shall study Che's diary in Bolivia.
      (personal notes)

Definite and definitive
Ex. I want a definite answer.
      (clear, explicit)
   The jury gave a definitive sentence.
      (decisive, final)

Dead and die
Ex. They found the man dead. (adjective)
He died of a sudden disease. (verb)

Divers and diverse
Divers: several, various, more than one.
Ex. There were divers articles offered for sale.
Diverse: different in character, unlike.
Ex. Their opinions were completely diverse.

Let go and Let's go
Ex. Please, let go, it's useless.
(Don't hold me)
Let's go to the ball tonight!
(invitation)

Freedom and liberty
Ex. I want to enjoy my freedom.
(individually)
We should struggle for our liberty.
(general concept)

Unable, disabled and incapable
Ex. She's most unable to do that.
(not capable)
That man is physically disabled.
(He has certain limitations)
The buddy is incapable to do his work.
(incompetent)

Conscious, conscientious and aware
Ex. She's not conscious of what she's saying.
(aware, knowing)
He is a conscientious worker.
(loyal to duty or principles)
We are aware of the danger.
(alert)

Memoirs and memories
Ex. She's writing her memoirs
  (biography, record of a person's own experience)
  Those memories still linger in my mind
  (reminiscences, impressions, recollection,
  remembrances)

Antic and antique
Ex. He's playing antics at her
  (silly tricks, capers)
  He has an antique gold watch
  (ancient, of times long ago)

Graduant and graduate
Ex. There's a meeting for graduants
  (students before receiving the diploma)
  The graduates held a party
  (students after finishing the studies)

Councillor and counsellor
Ex.. The councillor of the town visited us
  (Sp. concejal)
  You need to consult a counsellor
  (Sp. consejero, abogado)

Welfare and well-being
Ex. The state sees to the welfare of the people.
  (as an institution)
  The children can have a place for their care and
  well-being.
  (health condition)

Solve and resolve
Ex. I solved the problem.
  (Find a solution)
  We resolved to meet again on Tuesday.
  (Come to an agreement)

People is and people are
Ex. The People is struggling for the independence.
   (In Spanish: pueblo)
   The people are aware of their roles.
   (persons)

Excuse, pardon, forgive
Excuse: used of small faults.
Ex. Please, excuse my interruption.
Pardon: used of grave faults or crimes and usually
implies generosity towards a wrongdoer.
Ex. Pardon my lack of respect.
Forgive: used of an injury done to one's self or a debt.
Ex. Forgive my sins.

Compromise, commitment and engagement
Ex. There should be a compromise between the three
      nations.
      (agreement)
   The commitments of the unionists should be fulfilled.
      (Something we promise to carry out)
   We broke up our engagement and later made it up.
      (betrothal)

Struggle and fight
Ex. We struggle for peace.
      (Strain, make efforts for)
   The brave soldiers fought in Angola.
      (Wage a battle)

Mastermind and intellect behind
Ex. The murderer is the mastermind of this crime.
      (negative connotation)
   Jose Martí is the intellect behind the attack on the
   Moncada Garrison.
      (positive connotation)

Defender and defendant
Ex. The defender spoke on behalf of the defendant.
   (The former is the lawyer and the latter is the
   accused person).

Stained glass and tinted glass
Ex. I got a pair of specs made of tinted glass.
   (In Spanish: calobares)
   She has beautiful windows of stained glass.
   (In Spanish: vitrales)

Few and a few
Ex. Very few people came to the lecture.
   (scarcely any)
   Just a few days in bed will suffice.
   (some)

If he was and If he were
Ex. If John was at the meeting, he surely talked to the
   principal.
   (indicative).
   (Something may have been true in the past)
   If John were here, these things wouldn't happen.
   (subjunctive).
   (Implies doubt or indicates a circumstance contrary to
   fact)

Disinterested and uninterested
Ex. She is very disinterested.
   (Impartial, not seeking benefit for herself)
   She looks uninterested in class.
   (indifferent)

Leave me alone, let me alone and let alone
Ex. Leave me alone, please. I want to rest.
      (Allow me to remain by myself)
    Let me alone, I think I can do it.
      (Do not disturb or bother)
    I don't have a dime, let alone a buck!
      (even less)

Some and somewhat
Ex. We need some paint for the door. (adjective)
    I feel somewhat tired today.   (adverb)

Live, life and alive
Ex. I live in 456, Galiano street.   (verb)
    She bought live lobsters.   (adjective)
    She leads a peaceful life.   (noun)
    He is still alive.   (predicate adjective)

Round and around
Ex. We travelled round the ring.
      (circularly, in circumference)
    We went around the town.
      (on all sides, here and there)

To feel good and to feel well
    To feel good: to feel happy, to be in good spirits.
Ex. I feel good today.
    To feel well: to be in good health.
Ex. I'm feeling very well today.

To feel bad and to feel badly
    To feel bad: to feel ill or depressed.
Ex. I feel bad today.
    To feel badly: to have a bad sense of touch.
Ex. I'm feeling badly today so don't touch me!

Win, earn and gain
Win: refers to a contest, a prize, a game, a war
Ex. He won a prize.
Earn: refers to a salary, reputation, respect.
Ex. He earns a good salary.
     She has earned an evil reputation.
Gain: attention, knowledge, time, favor, experience, admission, prestige, recognition, weight and confidence.

Alone, lonely and solitary
Ex. I live alone.
        (without anyone around)
     I feel lonely today.
        (longing for companionship)
     He is a solitary man.
        (isolated, absence of companionship)

Obligate and oblige
Ex. The judge felt obligated to disqualify him.
        (moral or legal duty)
     I am much obliged to you for that.
        (grateful)

Each other and one another
Ex. They fell in love with each other.
        (two persons)
     The class exchanged the papers with one another.
        (more than two)

Isle and island
Ex. We flew to the Isle of Youth.
        (particular)
     An island is a portion of land surronded by water.
        (general)

Policy and politics
Policy: plan of action.
Ex. The policy of our boss is encouraging.
    (method of work)
Politics: business, art and science of government.
Ex. She doesn't know a word on politics.

Proposal and proposition
Ex. I have a proposal for the enterprise.
    (plan, scheme, offer).
    (A proposal may be accepted or rejected)
She made a preposition to think of.
    (statement, assertion, suggestion).
    (A proposition usually invites discussion)

Of course and off course
Ex. Of course I know her!
    (interjection)
The plane flew off course.
    (in the wrong direction)

Raise and rise
Ex. Raise your hand so as to speak.
    (transitive verb)
She rose and asked for the floor.
    (intransitive verb)

Lay and lie
Ex. Lay the books there.
    (transitive verb)
I like to lie on the grass.
    (intransitive verb)

Lose and loose

Ex. I lost the check as I was coming home.

    (verb)

That shirt is somewhat loose for me.

    (adjective)
    (not tight)

State and estate

Ex. The State cares for the elderly.

    (The body politic as organized for supreme civil rule
    and government)

 His real estate was confined.

    (properties)

Sensible and sensitive

Ex. You should be sensible with her.

    (reasonable)

She is very sensitive to criticism.

    (accutely affected by external impressions)

Critic, criticism and critical

Ex. The critics spoke favorably.

    (specialized persons)

 Constructive criticism is good and necessary.

    (remarks)

She made very critical remarks about the
misguided youngsters.

    (adjective)

Necessaries and necessities

Necessaries: things such as food and water without which
life cannot be maintained.

Ex. We have our necessaries satisfied.

Necessities: pressing needs, poverty, want.

Ex. Their necessities drove the refugees to seek help from
    the red cross, which provided them with the necessaries
    of life.

Temporal and temporary
Ex. Your discomfort will be temporal.
   (always occur)
   These avocados are temporary.
   (occasional)

Course and helping
Course: a part of a meal served at one time.
Ex. The main course was steak.
Helping: a portion served to a person at one time.
Ex. I want two helpings of rice.

Shall and will
SHALL is used for the future in the first persons singular and
   plural, but also to show a strong determination.
Ex. You shall go there.
WILL is used for the future in all persons except the first of
   the singular and plural, but in modern English, will is
   used to express future in all persons.
Ex. I will go there tomorrow.

Mayor and major
Ex. The mayor of the town died.
      (alcalde)
   The major addressed the audience.
      (comandante, mayor)

Attend, assist and treat
Ex. Did you attend the last class?
      (be present)
   The nurse assisted the wounded.
      (helped)
   The doctor treats the patients in the afternoon.
      (take care of)
   They treated me to a ball.
      (invite)

Specially and especially

Ex. This is a special mode.
    (unique)
    We came especially to see you.
        (fundamentally)

Used to, be + used to

Ex. I used to eat lots of sweets.
        (habitual action in the past)
    I am used to eating lots of sweets.
        (habitual action at present)

Defer and differ

Ex. We deferred the meeting because of your delay.
        (postpone)
    I differ from your opinion.
        (Do not share the same idea)

Greet and salute

Ex. They don't greet each other.
        (general salutation)
    The soldiers saluted the flag.
        (Said of the flag or military men)

Hire, lease and let

Hire: securing for temporary services or use by payment of a fee or wage
Ex. Hire a hall, a typist, a car.
Lease: to give or take the use of lands or buildings.
Ex. He leased me an apartment.
Let: to give the use of a room, land building, in return for regular payment.
Ex. He let me a room, a flat.

Use and usage
Ex. The use of benzyne is necessary for the mixture.
    (particular use)
    The usage of alcohol in wounds is widespread.
    (habitual and traditional)

Beat and win
Ex. I beat you in the checkers match. (an opponent)
    I won the contest. (a match, a prize, a competition)

Rob and steal
Ex. The thief robbed me of my money.   (a person)
    The burglar robbed the house.   (a place)
    She stole my wallet.   (a thing)

Hang, hanged; hang, hung
Ex. The man hanged himself.
    (committed suicide)
    I hung my clothes on the line.
    (To suspend a thing so that it is supported only from
    above)

Quiet and quite
Ex. Be quiet for a while!   (adjective)
    I don't quite understand you.   (adverb)

Classic and classical
Ex. I like classic music.
    (special, unique)
    This is a classical T-shirt.
    (model, historical)

Healthful and healthy
Healthful:good for the health.
Ex. It is very healthful to go to the beach.
Healthy: in good health.
Ex. These children are healthy because they eat healthy
    foods.

Devise, device, advise, advice, prophesy, prophecy
The words with S are verbs, while the others with C are nouns.
Ex. This is a wonderful device! Who devised it?
Take this piece of advice! He advised me to do it.
The witch prophesied a bad omen. I don't believe in his prophecies.

Discrete and discreet
Ex. The two models are discrete.
(separate, distinct)
He's a very discreet man.
(prudent)

Draft, draught and drought
Ex. You should hand in the draft.
(In Spanish: borrador)
The draught tumbled the vase.
(In Spanish: corriente de aire)
There is a terrible drought. (In Spanish: sequía)

Terrible and terrific
Ex. Cancer is a terrible disease.
(horrible)
She's terrific.
(awful)

Elder, eldest, older, oldest, oldster
Elder and eldest are used with persons of the same family.
Ex. My elder brother came to see me.
He's the eldest of the three of us.
Older and oldest are used with persons and things in general.
Ex. That book is older than this one.
Oldster is used as a noun, as an opposite to youngster.
Ex. There were many oldsters at the meeting.

Colonel and coroner
Ex. The colonel filed past the troops.
  (military man)
  The coroner analysed the case.
  (An officer whose chief function is to investigate any death not clearly due to natural causes)

Worry, concern and preoccupy
Ex. We are very worried about her behaviour.
  (personally)
  He is very much concerned about our affair.
  (not personal)
  She looks preocupied.
  (Thinking internally)

Mean, signify and purport
Ex. I mean what I say.
  (Meaning in general sense)
  What a fool says does not signify.
  (matter, have importance)
  The document purported to be official.
  (Have as its main idea)

Economic and economical
Ex. The lecture dealt with the economic crisis.
  (Related to economy)
  This is an economical restaurant.
  (cheap, not expensive)

Refuse and deny
Ex. I refuse to do it.
  (To express a determination not to do something)
  She refused the prize.
  (To decline to accept)
  She denied she had taken the money.
  (To declare not to be true)

Bring, take and fetch
Ex. Bring me the book, please.
        (To cause to come with oneself)
      Take the book with you.
        (tomar, llevar)
       Fetch me the glasses, please.
        (To go, get and bring from a place)

Pass and past
Ex. He passed the test succesfully.   (verb)
      She spoke about her past experiences. (adjective)
      She likes to speak about her past.   (noun)

So and such
Ex. She's so nice!   (very or extremely)
      She's so nice a person!
      She's such a nice person!

Business and busyness
Business: activities of buying and selling.
Ex. That shop does a very good business.
Busyness: action of being busy.
Ex. His busyness keeps him confined to that room.

Provisions and measure
Ex. We should make provisions for the future.
        (make arrangements beforehand)
      The police took measures with the mob that wanted to
      spoil the show.
        (legislative enactment)

True and truth
Ex. Did you say it is true?   (adjective)
      I want to know the truth.   (noun)

Beside and besides
Ex. Sit beside me.
  (close, nearby)
  I studied English and besides French.
  (in addition, moreover)

Photograph and photography
Ex. I've got a photograph of you.   (a picture)
  I like photography.   (art)

A picture of you, a picture of yours
Ex. They published a picture of you.
    (You are on it)
  I got a picture of yours.
    (One of the many you may have)

Made of, made from
Ex. This doll is made of cardboard.
    (one material)
  This cake is made from flour, sugar and eggs.
    (more than one)

Borrow, lend
Borrow and lend are opposites.
Borrow: to obtain a thing on the promise to return it.
Lend: to give the temporary use of something for a consideration.
Ex. I need to borrow ten pesos from you. Can you lend
    them to me?

Historic and historical
Ex. The book shows historic scenes of the town.
      (Important in history, very famous or very well known)
    We are using historical methods in the analysis.
      (Related to history, registered by history)
    I enjoy historical pictures.
      (historical events)

Exhibit, exhibition and display
Ex. The exhibit on computers drew large crowds.
        (part of an exhibition)
        The EXPOCUBA exhibition was a success.
        (exposition)
        There are several latest-fashion clothes on display.
        (smaller than an exhibition)

Expense and expenditure
Ex. The expense of the trip was slight.
        (less formal) (cost, charge)
        Military expenditures have been growing lately.
        (more formal spending)

Lightning, lightening and lighting
Ex. We saw a lightning during the storm.
        (atmospheric electrical discharge)
        We asked for lightening her work load this year.
        (Make less burdensome)
        The room had indirect lighting.
        (illumination)

Specie, species and speech
Ex. Long ago, the trade was carried out with specie.
        (coined money)
        He collects different species of fish.
        (kinds, classes, types)
        He made a speech of three hours.
        (Declaration; a form of communication in spoken
        language made by a speaker before an audience)

Dingy, dinghy
Ex. The room was dingy last week.
        (dirty-looking)
        We travelled in a dinghy.
        (small boat)

Ingenious and ingenuous
Ex. He is very ingenious for that sort of thing. (clever)
She looks an ingenuous girl.   (frank)

Rain and rein
Ex. The rain didn't let me go to the party.
(Water in drops falling from the sky to the earth).
I took the horse by the reins.
(A long, narrow strap fastened to the bridle by which a rider guides a horse or another animal)

Pair and pare
Ex. I bought a pair of shoes.   (a set of two)
We pared an apple before eating it.   (to trim)

Need and necessitate
Ex. I need twenty bucks.
(Denotes lack of something)
We necessitate a secretary for the staff.
(require, precise)

Able and capable
Ex. He is capable to work 16 hours a day.
(He has a potential but undeveloped power)
Erna is able to speak 6 languages.
(She has a developed power)

Pain and pane
Ex. I can't tolerate this pain. (suffering)
The pane is broken.   (glass part of window)

Breath and breathe
The first one is a noun and the second one is a verb. So we have:
Ex. I feel your breath close to me.
(Air inhaled and exhaled in respiration)
Breathe deeply and you'll feel better.
(to respire)

Bath and bathe
Again, the former is a noun and the latter is a verb:
Ex. I'd like to take a bath.
        (Washing of the body)
    We like to bathe in the sun.   (verb)

After and afterwards
Ex. We went to the movies and afterwards entered the
        cafeteria.
        (later)
      We went to the movies and after that, we went to the
      cafeteria.
        (subsequent to)

Admittance and admission
Ex. Admittance is not allowed to animals.
        (limited to letting into a particular place)
      The poor have no admission in this center.
        (privilege is involved)

Acceptance and acceptation
Ex. He received the acceptance for the scholarship.
        (Act of receiving or taking)
      We don't know about the acceptation of that word
      yet.
        (General acceptation of a word or usage)

Appliance and application
Ex. I want to buy electric appliances for my home.
        (electric household)
      I filled the application for the fellowship.
        (form, model)

Monograph and monography
Ex. You must write a monograph about you for tomorrow.
      (An account or description of a thing)
      Among the different pictures, we saw a beautiful
      monography in the gallery.
      (Kind of drawing in black and white)

**Specialty, speciality, specialization, specialist,
specialistic and specialize**
Ex. His specialty is Neurology.
      (field of study)
      The speciality of the restaurant is Donuts.
      (peculiarity, main feature)
      We work on the specialization of out technicians.
      (process)
      He is a specialist in that subject.
      (person)
      She works with a specialistic viewpoint.
      (related to a specialist)
      My son would like to specialize in surgery.   (verb)

Desert and dessert
   Desert can be both a noun and a verb.
Ex. The days in the desert were a trial by fire for us. (noun)
      Do not desert me now that I need you most.   (verb)
      (abandon)
      Dessert is a noun and means the course we have after
      any meal.
Ex. I'd like ice cream for dessert.

Volunteer and voluntary
Ex. I volunteered to go to Angola.   (verb)
      We need two volunteers for the dramatization.
      (persons)
      We must do some voluntary work.   (adjective)

Imply, implicate and involve
Imply: express indirectly, suggest.
Ex. The meaning of that sentence is implied.
    (inferred, suggested)
Implicate: entangled, show to have a part or be connected.
Ex. They implicated the plot of the play.
Involve: include, complicate.
Ex. Housework involves washing, cooking, cleaning,
    etcetera.
    He is involved in the crime.

Caution and precaution
Ex. The medicine has a caution which is not to drink more
    than two pills a day.
    (warning)
    He acted with precaution.
    (carefully)

Civil and civilian
Ex. The Civil War was something tragic.
    (Of or consisting of citizens)
    The man wore civilian clothes.
    (not a soldier)

Disposal and disposition
Ex. I am at your disposal.
    (Available to someone)
    She has always been at his disposition.
    (Under someone's orders)

Story and history
Ex. Children like to be told stories before going to sleep.
    (tales)
    History will condemn them.
    (Series of facts related among themselves)

Point at, point to
Ex. It's rude to point at people.
  (with the finger)
Fidel pointed to the misbehaviour of the culprits.
  (verbally)

Consist of and consist in
Ex. The house consists of two stories. (formed by)
  It consists in a new theory. (Is based on)

Seminar and seminary
Ex. The seminar is slated for Tuesday.
  (meeting, class)
  The monks and nuns live in a seminary.
  (religious school)

Prosthesis and prothesis
Ex. She has a prosthesis but no one realizes that.
  (Addition of an artificial part to supply a defect of the
   body)
  A prothesis is the addition of a phoneme or syllable at
  the beginning of a word.

Meet someone and meet with someone
Ex. I want you to meet Mr. Gómez.
  (Introduce a person)
  She met me at the corner.
  (accidentally)
  Fidel met with the delegates at the airport.
  (A meeting prepared beforehand)

Costume and custom
Ex. She wore a nice costume at the mascarade. (disguise)
  He has the custom of drinking too much. (habit)

Racism and racialism
Ex. We fight against racism, colonialism and any kind of
    exploitation.
        (Dealing with discrimination with race)
    In the United States there is a constant racialism.
        (rivalry among races)

In the hospital and at the hospital
    In the hospital
Ex. She was in the hospital for a week.
        (hospitalized)
    At the hospital
Ex. She was at the hospital to see her friend. (paying a visit)

Intense and intensive
Ex. I like intense colors.
        (strong)
    He needs an intensive treatment.
        (complete)

Scientific and scientist
Ex. He was a renowned scientist.   (person)
    She works in a scientific center.   (adjective)

Mix and mingle
Ex. To my mind, you shouldn't mix those substances.
    He is that kind of person who likes to mingle with
    anyone.
        (social intercourse)

Mechanical and mechanic
Ex. The functioning of the apparatus is mechanical.
        (Dealing with mechanics)
    He's a good mechanic.
        (person)
    That exercise is very mechanic.
        (repetitive, automatic)

Produce and product
Ex. We received some produce from Brazil.
    (agricultural products)
    We hope to produce new equipment for medicines.
    (verb)
    It's necessary to get a few products from Bulgaria.
    (in general)

Appearance and apparition
Ex. His personal appearance is clusmy.
    (aspect)
    The appearance of that drug in the market was a
    success.
    (Act of act of appearing to the eye, mind or public)
    She claims to have seen an apparition last night.
    (a ghost)

Unit and unity
Ex. The unit is made up of twelve items.
    (A single thing or group regarded as an individual)
    We struggle to obtain the unity.
    (oneness, union)

Chorus and choir
Ex. The ICRT chorus sang a lovely song.
    (in the theatre)
    The choir sang a hymn.
    (at church or at school)

Brothers and brethren
Ex. He has got three brothers.
    (family)
    The brethren gathered together for the mass.
    (Members of fraternal organization)

Exploit and explode
Ex. The ship exploded in the sea.
   (burst)
   The exploitation of man by man should disappear.
   (selfish utilization, utilize for profit)

Union and syndicate
Ex. There's a meeting of the union tonight.
   (workers)
   The Syndicate has a meeting today.
   (Belonging to the Mafia, in America)
   (In England means Union too)

Moral and morale
Ex. They all have a moral support form the people.
   (adjective)
   The moral teaching of the story is very educative.
   (adjective) (moraleja)
   The morale of Cuban troops has always been present
   everywhere.
   (noun)

Human and humane
Ex. The human race is struggling to be each day better.
   (adjective)
   Her humane feelings show what kind of person she is.
   (adjective)
   (Related to tenderness, compassion for the suffering)

Material and matériel
Ex. The material of the table is not up to snuff.
   (What it is made from)
   We brought some matériel for the minibrigade.
   (Aggregate of things, needed in any business, or
   equipment in general)

Council and counsel
Ex. The council resolved to meet next week.
    (assembly or meeting)
   She's looking for a good counsel.
    (advice)
    (Given as a result of consultation of a lawyer)

Mantle and mantel
Ex. She has a beautiful mantle.   (cloak)
    Put that vase on the mantel.   (shelf)

Stationary and stationery
Ex. The speceship remained stationary for two hours.
    (static)
   I dropped at the shop to get some stationery.
    (writing materials)

Egoism and egotism
Egoism: opposite of altruism.
Ex. He has always had a big egoism with his family.
    (wants all for himself)
    (philosophical notion that a person can prove nothing
    beyond the existence of his own mind)
   His egotism is disgusting.
    (showing off, praising about himself)
    (inflated vanity or preoccupation with the self)

Principal and principle
Ex. Go and see the principal of the school. (director)
    The principles of Physics are elementary for the solution
    to that problem.

Main and principal
Ex. Go ahead and turn at the main street.
    (great, important, big, chief)
    The principal thing for your cure is not to smoke.
    (capital, cardinal, fundamental, essential)

Personal and personnel
Ex. She has personal problems.
    (related to persons)
    The personnel of the factory welcomed us
    enthusiastically.
        (A body of persons engaged in public service,
        or the personal staff of an organization)

Confound and confuse
Confound: to cause great surprise or confusion, disturb
greatly.
Ex. His new scheme confounded her.
Confuse: to cause someone to be uncertain, unable to think
clearly.
Ex. All that mess confused the child.

Depreciate and deprecate
Ex. The price of those goods was depreciated.
    (lowered)
    The jury deprecated the final thesis.
        (To express disapproval)

Kind and sort
Ex. That kind of material is good for your book.
        (condition or quality)
    She is very kind-hearted.
        (condition)
    What sort of paper is this?
        (type or nature)

Enough, sufficient and adequate
Enough: satisfying a desire, or meeting a want.
Ex. I have enough wine, thanks.
Sufficient: completely fulfilling a proposed end or purpose.
Ex. The evidence was sufficient to convince me of his guilt.
Adequate: equal to a requirement.
Ex. Our supply of fuel oil is adequate for heating the house.

Shadow and shade
Shadow: shade made by some person, animal or thing.
Ex. The shadow of that man is still on my mind.
Shade: slight darkness afforded by something that cuts off light.
Ex. I like to sit under the shade of that tree.

Therefor and therefore
Therefor: for that, for it.
Ex. Five months abroad is the reward therefor.
Therefore: for that reason, because of that.
Ex. He passed in English and therefore got his degree.

Asleep and sleepy
Ex. Don't wake him up! He's fast asleep.
    (sleeping)
    He is sleepy all day.
    (Ready or inclined to sleep)

Recollect, recall, remember and remind
Recollect: to remember something past.
Ex. Do you recollect meeting her?
Recall: to remember.
Ex. I can't recall where she went.
Remember: to keep in memory, call back into the mind, to send greetings
Ex. I remembered posting the letter.
    Remember me to your parents.
Remind: to tell someone to remember a fact or something.
Ex. Remind me to call Susie up.

Biannual and biennial
Ex. The committee have a biannual meeting. (twice a year)
    This is a biennial event. (every two years)

Regime and regimen
Ex. The social regime in Chile is a dictatorship.
(Mode or system of rule or government)
He must go on a regimen to lose weight.
(diet)

Wish and desire
Ex. Make three wishes and throw a coin into the fountain.
(not practical)
I desire to make a trip to the C.I.S. this summer.
(a strong feeling)

File and archive
Ex. Keep this file in the closet.
(Set of papers kept in order)
We couldn't find the file in the archives.
(Place where files are kept)

Belong and pertain
Ex. That book belongs to me.
(ownership)
That bookcase pertains to the lounge.
(a part of, certain relationship with)

Meet, encounter and reunion
Ex. We resolved to meet after dark.
(general gathering)
The two men had an encounter with the police.
(involves angry people)
The graduates will hold a reunion next Sunday.
(usually said of graduates, students, etc.)

Peaceful and pacific
Peaceful: quiet, untroubled, not violent.
Ex. We struggle for peaceful coexistence.
Pacific: very calm and still.
Ex. There is a pacific environment in the room.

Motto, slogan and watchword
Ex. "Think before you speak" is a good motto.
(Brief sentence adopted as a rule of conduct)
"Service with a smile" is our stores slogan.
(Word or phrase used for advertising or promotion in clubs, political parties, etc.)
"Forward" is our watchword.
(A secret word that allows a person to pass a guard)

Weave and knit
Ex. They like to weave all day long.
(To form strips and threads into a fabric)
That woman knits quite well.
(To make a cloth by looping yarn or thread together with long needles)

Hymn and anthem
Ex. The crowd sang a hymn.
(A joyful song of triumph)
The people stood up while they sang the National Anthem.
(song of devotion or patriotism)

Broad and wide
Ex. He has broad shoulders.
(Full horizontal extent is considered)
There is a wide doorway in front of you.
(Unfilled space between limits)

Prise, price and prize
Prise (British): to raise, move or force with or as with a lever.
Ex. The officer prised the box open.
Price: sum or amount of money or its equivalent for which anything is bought, sold or offered for sale.
Ex. The price of that machine is much too high for us.
Prize: reward of victory or superiority, as in a contest or competition.
Ex. She got a prize in the competition.

Till, until, up to
Till and until have the same meaning, denote time.
Ex. We will wait till (until) they come.
Up to denotes space.
Ex. You should read from this page up to here.

Attend and tend
Though synonymous in certain cases, see the different connections.
Attend: give care, pay attention, be present.
Ex. I attended her to the door. (I showed her to the door)
    The doctor attended the wounded. (gave care)
    We attended the theatre. (were present)
Tend: commonly restricted to such cases as:
Ex. Tend the fire, tend the boiler, tend the machine, tend the
    cattle.

In time and on time
In time: for something.
Ex. I believe we are still in time for finding a solution.
On time: puntual.
Ex. We arrived on time for the performance.

Use, utilize and employ
Use: the most general of the three.
Ex. We have to use that tool.
Utilize: to make useful, to turn to profitable account.
Ex. We must utilize every means at our disposal.
Employ: to use the services of, to devote to a particular purpose.
Ex. To employ a person for a job.
    To employ time and energy in studying.

Still and yet

Still and yet have many closely related senses. Both often apply to past action or state extending to and including the present time.

Yet, with negative meaning, applies to completed action, often replacing a positive statement with still.

Thus: "He is not gone yet" is nearly the same as "He is still here"

Yet has a reference to the future that still does not share.

"We may be successful" implies that success may begin at any future time.

"We may be still successful" implies that we may continue to enjoy in the future such success as we are winning now.

Wound, injure and hurt

Ex. The enemy received severe wounds in the battle.
     (in a war)
   The woman was seriously injured.
     (in an accident)
   Only the driver was hurt.
     (When there is some pain)

Permit and permission

Permit can be a noun or a verb.
Ex. Do not permit him to stay here.   (verb)
   You need a permit to go in.
     (A written piece of paper)
   We all have permission to be around.
     (Formal oral consent or authorization)

Magician and wizard

Ex. The magician entertained the children.
     (One who plays tricks)
   The wizard of Oz was my favorite tale.
     (Man with magic power)

Through and throughout
Through: in at one end, and out at the other.
Ex. We walked through the cave.
Throughout: from end to end of, or in every part of.
Ex. I travelled throughout the campus grounds.

Competition and contest
Competition: effort to obtain something wanted by others, rivalry.
Ex. There is competition among business firms for trade.
Contest: fight, struggle, trial to see who can win.
Ex. A game or race is a contest.

Tale and story
Tale: a story of imaginary events, a lie, a false story.
Ex. She was reading tales of adventures.
    Don't tell me a tale (a lie).
Story: an account of events, real or imagined.
Ex. He likes telling the children funny stories.

Country and countryside
Country: nation, rural district.
Ex. We all fight for, our country.
Countryside: a particular section of a country, especially rural.
Ex. She lives in the countryside.

Wage and salary
Wage: price paid, usually by the day or a week to a laborer.
Ex. The laborer's wage will be paid today.
Salary: denotes a fixed periodical payment usually by the month or half-month, to persons employed in other than manual or mechanical work.
Ex. They found the doctor's salary.

If and whether
Whether + infinitive / if or whether + sentence
If: can be used either at the beginning of a clause or in the middle, joining because it is a conjunction.
Ex. If mother came, we would feel pleased.
  I don't know if mother will come today.
  I don't know whether mother will come today.
  I can't decide whether to call him or not.
  I can't decide if I should call him or not.

Fireplace, chimney and smokestack
Fireplace: that part of a chimney opens into an apartment and in which fuel is burned.
Ex. My house has a nice fireplace.
Chimney: a structure usually vertical containing a passage by which the smoke gases of a fire are carried out.
Ex. The chimney is not working.
Also part of that structure which rises above the roof.
Smokestack: a pipe for the escape of the smoke or gases of combustion in a steamboat, loco or building.
Ex. They built a smokestack in that building.

Emigrate, migrate, immigrate
Emigrate: Leave one own's country to settle in another.
Ex. The Spaniards emigrated from Spain many years ago.
Migrate: Move from one place to settle in another.
Ex. Most birds migrate to warmer countries in winter.
Immigrate: Come into a foreign country or region to live.
Ex. A host of Italians immigrated to Argentina.

Because of and due to
Because of: by reason of
Ex. I missed the show because of you.
Due to: owing or attributable to.
Ex. His failure was due to illness.

Sameness and similarity
Sameness: state of being exactly the same or identical.
Ex. There is a great deal of sameness between them.
Similarity: likeness or resemblance.
Ex. The similarity should not confuse you.

Stake and steak
Stake: a stout stick pointed for driving in the ground.
Ex. The farmer has a stake for ploughing the land.
Steak: a slice of meat.
Ex. We asked for steak in the restaurant.

Straight and strait
Straight: not crooked.
Ex. This is a straight road.
Strait: narrow, restricted.
Ex. Take a strait path next corner.

Strategy and tactics
Strategy: in warfare, refers to the planning and conducting of campaigns
Ex. We must follow this strategy to win.
Tactics: art of disposing troops or warships in single battles.
Ex. The tactics used in the guerrilla warfare was excellent.

Intend, attempt and try
Intend: to have it in mind to do, to be meant for.
Ex. I did not intend to make that mistake.
Attempt: to make an effort or to try.
Ex. I attempted to speak but it was useless.
Try: to attempt and do, experience.
Ex. Try doing more exercise.

Speech and discourse
Speech: act of speaking formally to a group of listeners.
Ex. The prime minister delivered a speech to all the people.
Discourse: general speech or writing.
Ex. We all read the discourse of the president.

Official and officer
Official: one who holds public office, especially one who exercises subordinate executive powers. (funcionario)
Ex. He is Customs official.
Officer: restricted to those in positions of command in uniformed services.
Ex. The officer brought the mail today.

Should and ought to
Should: used particularly with respect to appropriateness or fitness.
Ex. You should remove your hat on entering the house.
Ought to: implies more particular moral obligation.
Ex. We ought to support our aged parents if necessary.

Comic and comical
Comic: intended to be funny.
Ex. The clown amused the small fry with comic gestures.
Comical: something or someone unintentionally funny.
Ex. He looks comical with that shirt.

Spill and pour
Spill: fall or flow out, run, scatter. (unintentionally)
Ex.The milk was spilled on the table.
Pour: cause to fall or flow. (intentionally)
Ex. Will you please pour some coffee in my milk?

Dead and deceased
Dead: general term.
Ex. They brought the dead home.
Deceased: used of persons, but not of animals.
Ex. They found the deceased in the tub.

Remainder and reminder
Remainder: remmant, what is left.
Ex. If you take 3 from 8 the remainder is 5.
Reminder: something that causes one to remember
Ex. The man left a reminder on the windshield.

Between and among

Between is used for two persons or things, among for more than two.

Ex. I sat between Mary and Lucy.
I saw Peter among the crowd.
But: This is an agreement between England, France and Sweden.

Miss

Miss has several meanings.

Ex. I missed the bus because I arrived late.
(fail to get)
I missed my wife during my stay abroad.
(notice the absence of)
Let me introduce Miss Sullivan to you.
(girl, young woman)

Gourmand and gourmet

Gourmand: one who eats large quantities of food.

Ex. Jack is a gourmand.

Gourmet: one who eats large quantities of food but more fastidious.

Ex. You should prepare a good dinner. You know Peter is a gourmet.

Habit and custom

Habit: refers to the tendency to repeat a thing and specially to the individual.

Ex. I have the habit of smoking after drinking coffee.

Custom: refers to what one sees done as the result of habit and pertains to groups of persons rather than to individuals.

Ex. Cubans have the custom to eat a lot of fat.

Had better, had best and had rather (or would rather)
Had better and had best: indicate advisability.
Ex. You had better or (had best) see the doctor.
Had rather: indicates preferences.
Ex. I had rather stay than go.
   I would rather stay than go.

Farther and further
Farther: implies the idea of distance.
Ex. We walked farther into the woods.
Further: used figuratively, meaning additional.
Ex. Do you have any further questions?

Award and reward
Award: result of a considered decision.
Ex. A medal was awarded to the best speller in the class.
Reward: recompense or pay for good or evil done.
Ex. He was given a car as a reward.

Genious and genus
Genious: extraordinary ability or one who has such ability.
Ex. Peter is a genious.
Genus: class or kind.
Ex. This is a genus of a family of bulbous herbs.

Though and although
Though: in spite of the fact that.
Ex. We lost the game though we tried to win.

Although: even though.
Ex. Although he was warned, he persisted in his scheme.

As far as and so far as
As far as: expresses distance.
Ex. We went as far as the border.
So far as: implies limitation.
Ex. So far as I know, he's an outgoing man.

Assay and essay
Assay: to make a trial or an experiment.
Ex. We made an assay on ozone.
Essay: to make an intellectual or bodily effort.
Ex. The last essay has been his best.

Wander and wonder
Wander: to go aimlessly, without any intention.
Ex. We wandered through the woods all day long.
Wonder: to ask oneself, to be curious about.
Ex. I wonder what's become of Sally.

Design and designate
Design: to prepare the preliminary plans for a work.
Ex. She designed that project.
Designate: to name, entitle, nominate, appoint, assign.
Ex. He was designated for that post.

Chapter 2
Misleading Words

Some words are often confused and misused. Among the principal terms most commonly mistaken are the following:

Hardly: barely, not quite.
Ex. I had hardly time to study my lesson.

Lately: a short time ago. Recently.
Ex. I haven't seen Lucy lately.

Learly: almost, closely.
Ex. The bus nearly hit you! You'd better be careful.

Badly: desperately, urgently.
Ex. I need a tranquilizer badly.

Likely: probable, probably.
Ex. It is likely that he drops around today.

Presently: later.
Ex. We will do this job presently.

Eventually: in the end, finally.
Ex. You'll get the pronunciation of English eventually.

Conversely: if or when turned the other way around.
Ex. Six is more than five, cenversely, five is less than six.

Noisome: stinky.
Ex. That room is a noisome place.

Chapter 3
Idioms

Idioms are combinations of words with a special meaning that cannot be inferred from its separate parts. Idioms are a very important part of the English language.

Some important idioms and collocations are the following:

To die hard: tardar en morir.
    Ex. She's an old bag who dies hard.

When all is said and done: a fin de cuentas.
    Ex. When all is said and done, he won't understand it.

To take a chance on: arriesgarse.
    Ex. We have to take a chance and go there.

To hold water: ser válido.
    Ex. This agreement holds water until December.

As it were: por así decirlo.
    Ex. We studied, as it were, all day long.

To put to sleep (an animal): sacrificar un animal.
    Ex. Ubre Blanca was put to sleep.

To stick out like a sore thumb: señalarse.
    Ex. Don't stick out like a sore thumb.

At the beck and call: a entera disposición.
    Ex. I am at your beck and call.

In a row: consecutivamente.
    Ex. He has been a vanguard worker for five years in a row.

To hail from: provenir de.
    Ex. He hails from Guantánamo.

At the crack of dawn: al amanecer.
Ex. I got up at the crack of dawn.

To call quits: abandonar, marcharse.
Ex. When the meeting finished, I called quits.

To ring a bell: sonarle a uno, serle familiar.
Ex. Her name rings a bell to me.

To sponge: vivir de gorra.
Ex. Whenever he drops around here, he likes to sponge.

To be broke: arruinado.
Ex. I am broke until I get paid.

Get-at-able: asequible.
Ex. This is a very get-at-able book.

Let's call it a day: terminemos.
Ex. Let's call it a day and go.

All over the world: por todo el mundo.
Ex. That song was heard all over the world.

For fun, for the fun of it: por gusto, en vano.
Ex. We did it for the fun of it.

For sheer delight: por puro gusto.
Ex. I took French classes for sheer delight.

Get a kick out of: hallar placer en.
Ex. I get a kick out of singing.

At the drop of a hat: inmediatamente.
Ex. I did it at the drop of a hat.

In state: en capilla ardiente.
Ex. The body was lying in state.

Get the hang of it: cogerle el golpe.
　　Ex. When you get the hang of it, you'll find it easier.

See to it: ocuparse de, velar por.
　　Ex. You must see to it that the baby is well fed and looked
　　　　after.

Get away with: salirse con la suya.
　　Ex. At the end I always get away with it.

Pick on someone: cogerla con alguien.
　　Ex. Please, stop picking on me!

To come to: volver en sí.
　　Ex. She came to a day later.

Run out of: acabarse algo, terminarse algo.
　　Ex. I ran out of money.

I can't bear it: soportar, tolerar.
　　Ex. I can't bear this noise.

One good turn deserves another: un favor merece otro.
　　Ex. You should keep in mind one good turn deserves
　　　　another.

Mind you!: téngalo presente.
　　Ex. Mind you!, this is the last time I say it to you.

For one: al menos.
　　Ex. I, for one, don't know how to speak Japanese.

To pass away: to kick the bucket: morir.
　　Ex. He passed away at 7 o'clock.

To bum: picar (cigarros, fósforos, etc.).
　　Ex. He's always bumming cigarettes.

A blow by blow account: detallado.
Ex. He made a blow by blow account of the problem.

To hit the sack: irse a dormir.
Ex. I hit the sack at 9 p.m.

To jump the gun: adelantarse.
Ex. Let's jump the gun and start just now.

Clear cut: bien definido.
Ex. We need clear cut conditions for the work.

All-encompassing: que abarca o incluye todo.
Ex. We need an all-encompassing report about that.

Every other day: días alternos.
Ex. We have classes every other day.

On an equal footing: de tú a tú.
Ex. They deal with each other on an equal footing.

Up to snuff: de la calidad requerida.
Ex. The service is not up to snuff.

To be past everything: estar cumplido, dar, importar lo mismo una cosa que otra.
Ex. I am past everything and don't care what they think of me.

When it comes to: cuando se trata de.
Ex. When it comes to drinking, he's a heavy drunkard.

On labour: de parto.
Ex. She was on labour at 6 a.m.

It pays: vale la pena.
Ex. It pays to see the show.

To boil down to: se resume en.
Ex. The whole thing boils down to this.

A pipedream: sueño imposible.
Ex. What you want is a pipedream.

Every bit a father: todo un padre.
Ex. He's every bit a father with his sons.

All-round: integral.
Ex. He's an all-round man.

Contingent on: sujeto a.
Ex. He lives contingent on the people.

To broach: sacar a relucir.
Ex. I want to broach an aspect.

To make a clean slate of/to wipe the slate clean: borrón y
cuenta nueva.
Ex. We should forget our debts and make a clean slate of
it.

To vouch for: responder por.
Ex. I vouch for her.

Soft pedaling: no hacer énfasis en algo.
Ex. He made a soft pedaling on the problem.

By the cartload: en cantidades industriales.
Ex. He has dresses by the cartload.

Bent on: resuelto a.
Ex. Cuba is bent on becoming a medical power.

Dyed-in-the-wool: acérrimo.
Ex. He is a dyed-in-the-wool enemy of smoking.

Far death: muerte natural.
Ex. He died of far death.

To develop a soft spot: coger cariño a.
Ex. He took a soft spot towards her.

To come to grips: enfrentarse a.
Ex. The meeting came to grips with all wrongdoings.

Slated for: programado para.
Ex. The show was slated for Monday.

To cut corners: alcanzar una meta rompiendo las normas.
Ex. We must not cut corners in this stage.

To give a boost: dar un impulso, dar calor a.
Ex. We gave a boost to the work.

To bear the brunt: llevar el peso.
Ex. She bears the brunt of the house.

To make a strong pitch: convencer a alguien por la palabra.
Ex. We have to make a strong pitch.

To stand someone up: dejar plantado, embarcado.
Ex. She stood me up in the date.

To bear down: apretar, llevar recio.
Ex. We have got to bear down on the lazy people.

Up a notch: un tanto.
Ex. The song raised the enthusiasm up a notch.

Until the wee hours: hasta altas horas.
Ex. I studied until the wee hours.

Crack: de primera calidad.
Ex. This is a crack collective.

A crackdown: lucha a muerte.
Ex. We should carry out a crackdown on crime.

Merchant man: barco mercante.
Ex. We sailed in a merchant man.

Man of war: buque de guerra.
Ex. That is a man of war.

Can't help it: no poder evitarlo.
Ex. I can't help crying when I watch that film.

Help yourself: sírvase usted mismo.
Ex. You can help yourself to sweets and cookies.

To have/ask for the floor: pedir la palabra.
Ex. I want to have the floor.

Have a skeleton in the cupboard: tener un secreto oculto.
Ex. She has a skeleton in the cupboard and nobody knows
it.

Look forward to: esperar con ansiedad.
Ex. I am looking forward to my vacations.

Catch up with: empatarse con, ponerse a la par de.
Ex I must catch up with the group because I missed many
classes.

On the ticket of: con la anuencia o permiso de.
Ex. I did it on the ticket of you.

I mean it!: lo digo en serio!.
Ex. I'm serious about this; I mean it!

To start from scratch: comenzar de cero.
Ex. This course starts from scratch.

Out of the blue: de la nada.
   Ex. Did this come out of the blue?

To settle for: conformarse con.
   Ex. She had to settle for the pink dress.

To pull one's leg: tomar el pelo.
   Ex. Are you pulling my leg?

The more... the better: cuanto más... mejor.
   Ex. The more you study, the better you'll come out in the
      test.

At large: en libertad.
   Ex. When the man was at large, he took revenge on her.

At length: al fin, por fin.
   Ex. We could find at length a place to spend the week end.

By far: con mucho, suficiente.
   Ex. She knows all that by far.

Horse sense: sentido común.
   Ex. That makes a lot of horse sense.

To make do: conformarse con.
   Ex. We will have to do with that amount.

More often than not: no pocas veces, regularmente.
   Ex. More often than not have I visited that place for some
      paper.

Beyond my ken: más allá de mis conocimientos.
   Ex. That is beyond my ken; I can't tell you an answer.

By leaps and bounds: a grandes pasos, rápidamente.
   Ex. The success in the economic plans can be seen by
      leaps and bounds.

If the cap fits, wear it: al que le sirva ...
   Ex. You are not involved in that problem but if the cap fits, wear it.

All hell broke loose: se armó la gorda.
   Ex. We left the party before all hell broke loose.

To take pains: esmerarse, poner cuidado en.
   Ex. We took pains in the work.

Straight from the horse's mouth: de buena tinta.
   Ex. I got the news straight from the horse's mouth.

A pony: un chivo (papel con notas para los exámenes).
   Ex. Lucy had a pony in her desk and the teacher got it.

Tickled to death: muy contento.
   Ex. Betty was tickled to death with the present.

To play second fiddle: ser plato de segunda mesa.
   Ex. This time I won't play second fiddle.

To come to terms: llegar a un acuerdo.
   Ex. We broke up and never came to terms.

To be out of the question: ser imposible.
   Ex. It's out of the question what you ask me.

A strong suit: plato fuerte (especialidad de uno).
   Ex. Mathematics is my strong suit.

To be cut out for: tener talento para algo.
   E.g. Peter was cut out for music.

To know the ropes: conocer a fondo, tener experiencia.
   Ex. She knows the ropes in her field.

Like father, like son: de tal palo, tal astilla.
　　Ex. It's not strange that Jack acts that way, imagine, like
　　　　father like son.

To be a plugger = a bunsen, a culture vulture: en lenguage
estudiantil: un mechado.
　　Ex. Tom is a plugger in the classroom.

Two of a kind: tal para cual.
　　Ex. Johnny and Mildred are two of a kind.

At best: cuando más, a lo sumo.
　　Ex. We need at best three bottles of brandy.

After a fashion: hasta cierto punto.
　　Ex. That is, after a fashion, a good solution to the problem.

To make sport of: burlarse de.
　　Ex. They all were making sport of me.

To be a good (or bad) sport: ser buen (o mal) perdedor.
　　Ex. You must be a good sport when you fail.

To soft soap: adular, dar coba.
　　Ex. Don't soft soap me! I'm tired of all that.

Spick and span: limpio y ordenado.
　　Ex. She keeps her home spick and span.

The small fry: la gente menuda, la grey infantil.
　　Ex. There is a picture for the small fry on T.V.

To turn the tables: los pájaros tirándole a la escopeta.
　　Ex. You are turning the tables on me! Who do you think
　　　　you are?

To be a milestone: acontecimiento relevante.
  Ex. The discovery of that vaccine was a milestone in the
     field of To rough it: pasar trabajos, vicisitudes.
  Ex. We had to rough it in our holidays this year.

Safe and sound: sano y salvo.
  Ex. We were safe and sound after the accident.

To rain cats and dogs: llover a cántaros.
  Ex. Yesterday it rained cats and dogs.

To go Dutch treat: ir a la americana (pagar cada cual lo
suyo).
  Ex. If we don't have much money we can go Dutch treat.

To be meant for something or someone: nacer para algo (o
alguien).
  Ex. Peter says Lucy was meant for him.

To cut the figure of: hacer el papel de.
  Ex. You are cutting a bad figure in all this mess.

Make yourself scarce: vete con disimulo.
  Ex. You'd better make yourself scarce before they realize.

To follow suit: imitar, hacer lo mismo.
  Ex. George began to sing and all the people followed suit.

To follow the flow: seguir la corriente.
  Ex. Don't discuss with her and follow the flow.

To keep abreast of something: estar al tanto de.
  Ex. We must keep abreast of the results of the test.

To have green fingers: tener buena mano.
  Ex. She has green fingers for everything she plants.

To see eye to eye: estar de acuerdo.
Ex. We all saw eye to eye with the minutes.

To try someone (a woman): en la norma cubana: enamorar, tratar de conquistar a una mujer.
Ex. He's been trying her all this time.

Better half: media naranja (esposa).
Ex. My better half doesn't like to gamble.

To pull strings for someone: usar influencias, tener palanca.
Ex. She said she had someone who pulled strings for her.

Not to mince matters: no tener pelos en la lengua.
Ex. I don't mince matters and I say what is wrong.

Up to the pretty: hasta el borde (de un vaso).
Ex. Fill the glass up to the pretty, please.

Neck or nothing: todo o nada.
Ex. You should choose: neck or nothing.

Head or tail: a cara o cruz.
Ex. Let's toss a coin and choose head or tail!

To get browny points: ganarse puntos
     (ganarse el favor de alguien).
Ex. She's trying to get browny points with him.

To make ends meet: irla pasando con lo que se tiene.
Ex. How do you manage to make ends meet with your salary?

To get by: irla pasando, ir viviendo.
Ex. How are you? Well, I get by.

Once in a blue moon: de Pascuas a San Juan.
Ex. He visits her once in a blue moon.

For the time being: por el momento.
Ex. We are working for the time being on a new project.

For good: para siempre.
Ex. Are you going to stay here for good?

To burn the midnight oil: quemarse las pestañas.
Ex. I was all my life burning the midnight oil to be a competent professional.

Hand and glove: ser uña y carne.
Ex. Bob and Lewis are hand and glove (part and parcel).

Everything under the sun: de todo como en botica.
Ex. In that shop you can find everything under the sun.

Piped-in music: música indirecta.
Ex. The hotel has piped-in music all day.
The same sauce with different gravy: el mismo perro con diferente collar.
Ex. That solution is the same sauce with different gravy.

To wax old: envejecer.
Ex. I'm waxing old each day.

A slip of the tongue: equivocarse al hablar confundiendo las palabras.
Ex. The speaker had a slip of the tongue and everybody started to laugh.

To give the cold shoulder: tirar un hielo (acoger con frialdad).
Ex. She gave me a cold shoulder yesterday.

To hold in store: deparar, tener reservado.
Ex. No one knows what destiny holds in store for us.

To bring down the house: to give a big hand: aplaudir.
Ex. The audience brought down the house.

To call a spade a spade: al pan, pan y al vino, vino.
Ex. Let's call a spade a spade and analyze things as they
should.

To take a fancy: antojarse, encapricharse de algo.
Ex. The child took a fancy to a toy and we had to buy it.

In a jiffy: inmediatamente.
Ex. We must do this in a jiffy.

To get the nod: dar el visto bueno.
Ex. The boss gave me the nod for the project.

In a nutshell: brevemente.
Ex. This is, in a nutshell, the report I bring.

To be at odds with: estar reñido con.
Ex. His attitude is not at odds with ours.

To have a sweet tooth for: ser goloso.
Ex. The children have a sweet tooth for candies.

To wear a couple of hats: hacer varios trabajos.
Ex. The doctor is wearing a couple of hats in these days.

A wet blanket: un aguafiestas.
Ex. John is a wet blanket when he goes to parties.

To be of age: ser mayor de edad.
Ex. Mary will be of age next week.

An apple polisher: a boot licker: un tracatán, chicharrón.
Ex. Tom is the apple polisher of the teacher.

A blue-eyed boy: the teacher's pet: alumno favorito del
maestro.
Ex. Peter is the blue-eyed boy of the class.

You can't beat: no puede haber mejor cosa que.
   Ex. You can't beat enjoying a holiday in Varadero.

To be cranky: matraquilloso.
   Ex. Grandma is getting cranky lately.

To go for a spin: dar una vuelta (en vehículo).
   Ex. Let's go for a spin and see the city.

To cluck the tongue: to go tsk: freir huevos (protestar con la boca).
   Ex. He's always clucking the tongue at me!

To feel ten feet tall: sentirse muy feliz
   Ex. I feel ten feet tall today because my son got his degree.

To get fussy: coger lucha.
   Ex. Don't get fussy about that. It will be solved soon.

To talk turkey: hablar de negocios, de dinero.
   Ex. Let's talk turkey, it's high time for that.

To have a notion to: tener deseos de.
   Ex. I have a notion to drinking coffee.

It's a quirk of nature: un capricho de la naturaleza.
   Ex. It seems a quirk of nature that tree with that shape.

A freak of nature: un aborto de la naturaleza.
   Ex. He's a freak of nature.

A hole-in-the-wall industry: chinchal.
   Ex. He used to work in a hole-in-the-wall workshop.

A shrink: un psiquiatra.
   Ex. He has a date with the shrink today.

To catch on: prender, coger fuerza, tomar auge.
Ex. The latest fashion caught on the youth at once.

On a par with: a la altura de.
Ex. This festivity is on a par with the occasion.

Below par: por debajo de.
Ex. She finished her training below par.

On our toes: atento, alerta.
Ex. We should be on our toes.

To gear towards (for): estar listo (para).
Ex. You should gear yourself for speaking.

At the helm of: al frente de.
Ex. The manager is at the helm of the enterprise.

A twist of fate: un golpe de suerte.
Ex. His triumph was a twist of fate.

To harp on: hacer énfasis.
Ex. The course harps on ear training and communication.

To have a cat boiled: quererse aprovechar de lo que uno regala.
Ex. She gave him a present and now is having a cat boiled.

In tandem with: venir convoyado con.
Ex. I bought this perfume in tandem with the rouge.

It's not amiss: no está de más.
Ex. It's not amiss to recall this item.

Booby prize: premio flaco.
Ex. She got the booby prize in the contest.

To plug oneself: hacerse propaganda uno mismo.
Ex. He likes to plug himself.

Few and far between: pocos, escasos.
Ex. Skilled skippers are few and far between.

To juggle (schedules, activities): jugar con.
Ex. It's not easy to juggle schedules.

To have a craving for: tener un antojo (de una mujer embarazada).
Ex. My wife had a craving for oranges.

To rule out: descartar.
Ex. We can't rule out this possibility.

Top-notch: excelente.
Ex. This is a top-notch film.

Over the counter: sin receta médica.
Ex. They sell drugs over the counter.

To be a wallflower: ser patón (no bailador).
Ex. Johnny is a wallflower in the parties.

The also rans: perdedores.
Ex. Industriales were the also rans in the championship.

Mind over matter: triunfo de la voluntad y el coraje sobre el dolor.
Ex. This is a case of mind over matter.

The spitting image: el vivo retrato.
Ex. His son is the spitting image of his father.

To be one too many: sobrar, estar de más.
Ex. You are one too many in this group. Move!.

It shows: se nota.
Ex. It shows she is madly in love.

To fill her hope chest: habilitación de boda.
Ex. She's filling her hope chest.

It meets the eye: salta a la vista.
Ex. It meets the eye she likes him.

You send me = You thrill me: me emocionas!.
Ex. You send me when you sing that song.

To be a teetotaler: abstemio, no tomador.
Ex. He's always been a teetotaler.

At a stretch: de un golpe, de una vez.
Ex. He drank the glass at a stretch.

To play truant = to play hookey: no ir a la escuela.
Ex. The kid decided to play truant and went fishing instead.

A field day: un día de éxito.
Ex. It was a field day for all of us.

To make passes at (a woman): decir piropos a (una mujer).
Ex. He made some passes at her in the party.

A catch-22 situation: situación difícil.
Ex. We were in a catch-22 situation.
(from the book by Joseph Heller, 1961).

A flat joke: chiste de mal gusto.
Ex. It was a flat joke.

A practical joke: broma pesada.
Ex. He cracked a practical joke on her.

To be stranded = to be left in the lurch: dejar embarcado.
Ex. They left me in the lurch yesterday.

Once too often: con exceso.
Ex. He repeats that once too often.

To have a bun in the oven: dar un mal paso.
Ex. Everybody says she has a bun in the oven.

To give a cop out: dar una evasiva, dar de lado.
Ex. She gave me a cop out.

The nitty gritty: fundamentos básicos.
Ex. This is the nitty gritty of the lesson.

To shoot in the dark: no acertar, tirar piedras.
Ex. You are shooting in the dark today.

To be in the back burner: ser de menor importancia.
Ex. That item is in the back burner in the meeting.

Off the beaten track: fuera de lo común
Ex. His behaviour is off the beaten track

There and then: Ahora mismo
Ex. He arrived there and then

All your geese are swans: Sobrevalorar nuestras ideas
Ex. He always thinks that all his geese are swans

All your swans are geese: Todas tus esperanzas han desaparecido
Ex. I think all your swans are geese

Chapter 4
Hints on Pronunciation

It is no secret for anyone that English shows a lack of correspondence between phonemes and graphemes, id est, between sounds and letters.

We will not take a biased position as to whether this is a chaotic fact or not, because we prefer to leave it to your own judgement; however we do want to give a few examples of some irregularities that would wrack the brains of any student or specialist of the English language, and to top it all, to illustrate this with a poem which comprises some of these irregularities.

How would you pronounce the following words?

Quay
Queue
Shammy
Sean
Gilbert
Tier
Pall Mall
Suet
Skein
Manor
Rational
Plumber
Climber
Cambridge
Knowledge
Gauge
Evil
Devil
Steak
Streak
Bugle

Orator
Belfry
Cupboard
Gaol
Colonel
Coroner
Jeopardize
Leopard
Forehead
Sword
Paean
Pageant
Arkansas
Gloucester
Leicester
Worcester
Sew
Victuals
Lough
Font
Posthumous
Honest
Homage
Roosevelt
Drought
Bough
Dough
Corps
Plaque
Herb
Heir
Butcher
Butler
Bucket
Soccer
Eulogy
Hiccough
Cough

Naked
Wicked
Wretched
Aisle
Stephen
Thomas
Uncouth
Tomb
Reuter
Demon
Plaid
Barbed
Danish
Spanish
Climber
Midget
Budget
Shepherd
Layer
Ewe
Fabric
Graham
Worm
Seismic
Heifer
Bosom
Quasi
Awry
Dour
Evans
Tapestry
Séance
Owl
Thorough
Werewolf
Zealot
Yosemite
Ghoul

Scruples
Bhaer
Quency
Cleanse
Reading (City in Pennsylvania with over 111,000 inhabitants).
Zoological
Schism
Blackguard
Archive
Archipelago
Flaccid
Chimera
Lichen
Viscount
Thyme
Machination
Schism
Reich
Phoebe
Phoenix
Deirdre

Some other suggestions should be taken into account regarding the following specific cases.

How would you pronounce these words?

Mature, maturity
Maturate, maturation
Nature
Natural
Hero
Heroine
Wide
Width
Wise
Wisdom
Sign
Signal
Misery
Miser
Nation
National
Pale
Pallor
Christ
Christen
Prophecy
Prophesy
Luxe
Luxury
Luxurious
Wild
Wilderness
Tyrant
Tyranny
South
Southern
Hide
Hideous

Rabid
Rabies
Pleasing
Pleasant
Prohibit
Prohibition
Satiate
Satiety
Inflamed
(In)flammable
Horizon
Horizontal
Apologize
Apology
Prime
Primer
Admire
Admirable
Compare
Comparable

In English some words have two different forms of pronunciation, depending on the meaning they convey.

Some examples are the following:

Read
Saw
Sow
Wind
Tear
Prayer
Lead
Gib
Row
Minute
Bow
Learned
Wear
Desert
Live
Sewer
Slaver
Buffet
Cleanly
Consummate
Divan
Does
Gill
Hinder
Intimate
Invalid
Lower
Precedent
Putting
Separate
Tarry
Worsted
Wound

Patent
Gallant
Bass
Dove
Number
Singer
Refuse
Lather

And now, take a look at this piece of poetry which summarizes to some extent what we have said:

I take it you already know:

Of tough and bough and cough and dough
others may stumble, but not you,
on hiccough, thorough, lough and through
well done and now you wish perhaps
to learn of less familiar traps.
Beware of heard, a dreadful word,
that looks like heard and sounds like bird,
and dead, it's said like bed, not bead,
for goodness sake, don't call it "deed",
watch out for meat and great and threat,
they rhyme with suite and straight and debt.
A moth is not a moth in mother,
nor both in bother, broth in brother,
and here is not a match for there,
nor dear and fear for bear and pear,
and then, there's dose and rose and lose,
just look them up-and goose and choose,
and cork and work, and card and ward,
and font and front, and word and sword,
and do and go, and thwart and cart,
come, come, I've hardly made a start,
a dreadful language, man alive,
I'd mastered it when I was five.

THE CHAOS

Dearest creature in creation,
Study English pronunciation,
I will teach you in my verse
Sounds like corpse, corps, horse and worse,
I will keep you, Susy, busy,
Make your head with great grow dizzy,
Tear in eye your dress you'll tear,
So, child, oh, hear my prayer.
Just compare heart, beard and heard,
Dies and diet, lord and word,
Sword and sward, retain and Britain,
(Mind the latter, how it's written)
Now I surely will not plague you
With such words as vague and ague,
But be careful how you speak,
Say break, stake, but bleak and streak,
Cloven, oven, how and low,
Script, receipt, show, poem, toe.
Hear me say, devoid of trickery:
Daughter, laughter and Terpsichore,
One, anemone, balmoral,
Kitchen, lichen, laundry, laurel,
Gertrude, German, wind and mind;
seem, napomone, mankind.
Billet does not sound like ballet,
Bouquet, wallet, mallet, chalet.
Blood and flood are not like food,
Nor is mould like should and would.
And your pronunciation is O.K.
When you correctly say croquet,
Rounded, wounded, grieve and sleeve,
Friend and fiend, alive and live,
Liberty, library, heave and heaven,
Rachel, ache, moustache, eleven,
We say hallowed but allowed,
People, leopard, towed but vowel.
River, rival, tomb, bomb, comb,

Doll and roll, and some and home.
Stranger does not rhyme with anger,
Neither does devour with clangour.
Soul but foul, and gaunt but aunt.
Query does not rhyme with very,
Nor does fury sound like bury.
Though the difference seems little,
We say actual, but victual.
Refer does not rhyme with deafer,
Feoffer does, and zephyr, heifer.
scenic, arabic, pacific,
Science, conscience, scientific,
Tour but our and succour, four,
Gas and alas and Arkansas.
Sea, idea, guinea, area,
Psalm, Maria but malaria.
Youth, south, southern, cleanse, clean,
Doctrine, turpentine, marine,
Say aver, but ever, fever,
Neither, leisure, skein, receiver,
Face but preface, but efface.
Phlegm, phlegmatic, ass, grass, bass.
Seven is right, but so is even,
Hyphen, roughen, nephew, Stephen,
Monkey, donkey, clerk and jerk,
Asp, grasp, wasp, and cork and work.
Won't it make you lose your wits,
Writing "groats" and saying grits?
It's a dark abyss or tunnel,
Strewn with stones; like rowlock, gunwale,
Islington, and Isle of Wight,
Housewife, verdict, indict.
Finally: which rhymes with enough,
Though, through, plough, cough or tough?
Hiccough has the sound of cup.
My advice is: Give it up!

Chapter 5
False Cognates

False cognates are words which resemble others in our mother tongue but have a different meaning. We have brought some examples of the most common false cognates we usually find in our daily conversation and reading.

Comprehensive: Integral

Tramp: vagabundo

Compass: brújula

Intoxicated: borracho

Extravagant: despilfarrador

Expedient: oportuno, conveniente

Suggestion: sugerencia

Fin: aleta

Library: biblioteca

Explicate: aclarar, desenredar

Discourse: plática, conversación

Motto: lema

Summary: resumen

Lechery: lujuria

Cigar: tabaco

Bracelet: pulso

Procure: conseguir, lograr

Publicize: divulgar

Suffocate: asfixiar

Actual: real

Dismay: congoja, desánimo

Disgrace: deshonra, oprobio, infamia

Facility: instalación

Commodity: artículo

Inauguration (of a president): toma de poder de un presidente

Pretend: fingir, hacer creer

Realize: darse cuenta

Exit: salida

Success: éxito

Bonus: prima (dinero)

Lecture: conferencia

Litter: camilla

Coroner: médico forense

Impregnable: inexpugnable

Crime: delito

Defendant: acusado

Resignation: renuncia

Assignation: cita con propósito sexual

Relative: pariente

Parent: padre

Ratoon: retoño de caña

Cocoon: capullo del gusano de seda.

Complexion: cutis

Parcel: paquete

Notice: fijarse, notar

Confectionery: confitería

Spade: pala

Forger: falsificador

Disparate: desigual, diferente

Embarrased: apenado

Deposition: declaración

Jug: jarra

Jar: pomo

Vase: jarrón

Resist: rehusar, negarse a

Casualty: bajas (en una guerra)

Rostrum: tribuna

Sympathy: pésame

Curator: celador (de un museo)

Compromise: acuerdo

Demand: exigir

Intend: proponerse

Attempt: intentar

Propaganda: desinformación

Scheme: plan, proyecto, trama

Asylum: manicomio

Fabric: tela, tejido

Sensible: razonable, sensato

Exciting: emocionante

Support: apoyar

College: universidad

Scholar: erudito, estudioso

Grass: hierba

Once: una vez

Quince: membrillo

Trip: viaje

Carpet: alfombra

Probation: libertad condicional

Salvage: salvamento

Sable: marta y su piel

Saber: sable

Mantel: repisa de chimenea

Introduce (a person): presentar a una persona

Gallant: valiente, intrépido

Miserable: infeliz, desdichado

Inhabitable: habitable

Traduce: difamar, calumniar

Disgust: asquear, repugnar

Practitioner: médico general

Dessert: postre

Demonstration: manifestación

Tambourine: pandereta

Adequate: suficiente

Self-sufficient: que se basta a sí mismo

Clerical: burocrático

Patron: comensal, cliente

Matron: jefa de enfermeras

Industry: laboriosidad, diligencia

Pan: cazuela

Premises: predios

Concourse: multitud de personas

Idiom: expresión idiomática

Dime: moneda de diez centavos

Dale: valle, cañada

Dinner: comida

Physician: médico clínico

Career: profesión

Blandish: adular, engatusar.

Grocer: bodeguero.

Large: grande

Portrait: retrato

Vine: enredadera

Collaborate: cooperar

Character: personaje

Resolve: llegar a una conclusión, acordar

Campus: patio o claustro de un colegio o universidad

Relevant: pertinente

Disorder: trastorno, alteración

Syndicate: asociación de capitalistas para emprender un negocio

Geneva: Ginebra

Presently: más tarde, después, luego

Gum: encía

Eventually: finalmente

Resume: reanudar (relaciones entre dos países)

Bigot: fanático

Scales: pesas, básculas, balanza

Utility: comodidad (de una casa)

Disgusting: asqueante, repugnante

Dependable: confiable

Molest: acosar (sexualmente)

Comprehensive: integral

Appreciate: agradecer

Transcendental: idealista, espiritual

Scandalous: vergonzoso

Actuation: operación, accionamiento

Reparation: pagar por gastos de accidente

Faction: bandos, grupos

Fabrication: mentira

Sauce: salsa

Chapter 6
Compounds

One of the characteristics of English is the capacity it has for forming compounds, that is, units which, though made up of two or more elements, each of which may be used as a separate term, are however, felt to be single words.

The written form of these compounds is somewhat arbitrary; sometimes they are written as one word and some other times as two words joined or not by a hyphen.

The semantic integrity of compounds is very often idiomatic in its character.

This means that the meaning of the whole is not a mere sum of its elements; since a compound is very often very different in meaning from the syntactic group formed by homonymous free forms.

There are, on the other hand, non-idiomatic compounds with a perfectly clear motivation.

Here the meanings of the constituents add up in creating the meaning of the whole, and name the referent either directly of figuratively.

Some examples of different compounds of several kinds are the following:

Dovetail: ensamblar

Cowlick: remolino (del pelo)

Deadline: plazo

Outline: plan general, esbozo, esquema

Hotline: hilo directo

Hotbed: foco (de vicios)

Sidekicks: compañeros de lucha

Blackout: apagón

Blackhead: espinilla

Brownout: oscurecimiento por baja del fluido

Nightmare: pesadilla

Blackmail: chantaje

Red-tape: burocratismo

Dead-end: callejón sin salida

Dead letter: algo que está escrito, pero que no se cumple

Dead lock: barrera, obstáculo, punto muerto

Shortcomings: deficiencias

Drawbacks: inconveniente

Catcalls: chiflidos de desaprobación en un acto público

Bronx cheers: trompetillas

Highlight: incidencias, cosa sobresaliente

Landmark: hito

Hallmark: marca de calidad

Hangover: rezago, resaca (de borrachera)

Windshield: parabrisas

Steadfast: constante

Castor oil: aceite ricino

Butterfly: mariposa

Overnight: de la noche a la mañana

Fortnight: quincena

Dropout: baja (académica)

Blueprint: proyecto, diseño, plan (terminado)

Stagehand: tramoyista

Mouthpiece: vocero

Layoff: despido (de obreros)

Earmark: destinar

Tenderfoot: novato

Pinpoint: entrar en detalle minucioso

Hairsplit: ser quisquilloso

Heartburn: acidez

Brainchild: fruto, engendro, producto

Absent-minded: distraido

Faint-hearted: cobarde

Down-hearted: abatido

Half-hearted: abúlico, apático

Weak-kneed: flojo de piernas

Level-headed: equilibrado

Pig-headed: tosudo, testarudo

Cool-headed: ecuánime

Far-flung: vasto, extenso

Skylight: claraboya

Headlong: temerario

Longshoreman: estibador

Longhand: letra cursiva

Shorthand: taquigrafía

Light-hearted: alegre

High-handed: despótico

Open-handed: dadivoso

Light-handed: mano blanda

Self-taught: autodidacta

Self-esteem: amor propio

Self-sacrifice: abnegación

Self-sufficient: independiente, que se autoabastece

Self-defense: autodefensa

Self-explanatory: que se explica por sí mismo

Self-appraisal: autovaloración

Self-determination: autodeterminación

Self-restraint: dominio de sí mismo

Self-reliant: que confía en sí mismo

Self-defeating: contraproducente.

Shop-worn: manido, gastado

Fed-up: harto

Push-ups: planchas (ejercicio)

Sit-ups: abdominales (ejercicio)

Air-tight: herméticamente cerrado

Water-tight: impermeable

Know-how: conocimiento total de algo

Well-to-do: adinerado

Part-time (job): contrata.

Full-fledged: completo, terminado, integral

Far-fetched: forzado, traido por los pelos

Far-reaching: trascendental

Deep-seated: arraigado

All-encompassing: que todo lo abarca

Tight-rope: cuerda floja

Chapter 7
Shortenings and Blendings

Shortenings

Word-building processes involve not only qualitative but also quantitative changes. Thus, derivation and compounding represent addition of, respectively, affixes and free stems to the underlying form.

Shortening, on the other hand, may be represented as a significant substraction, in which part of the original word is taken away.

The spoken and the written forms of the English language have each their own patterns of shortening; but as there is a constant exchange between both spheres, it is sometimes difficult to tell where a given shortening really originated.

As a type of word-building, shortening of spoken words, also called clipping is recorded in the English language as far back as the fifteenth century.

Since then it has grown more and more productive. Newly shortened words appear continuously; this is testified by numerous neologisms.

Shortened words may be classified according to whether the initial, final, or middle part of the word is cut off. As a result, we distinguish initial, final and medial clipping.

Some important shortenings taking into account their use are the following:

Chimp: chimpanzee	Flu: influenza
Photo: photograph	Phone: telephone
Bus: omnibus	Bra: brassiere
Pep: pepper	Comfy: comfortable
Howdy?: How do you do?	Frank: frankfurter
Ad: advertisement	Pram: perambulator
Lab: laboratory	Maths: mathematics
Perm: permanent wave	Mike: microphone
Loco: locomotive	Mac: mackintosh
Dorm: dormitory	Vet: veterinary,veteran
Doc: doctor	Fan: fanatic
Taxi: taximetercab	Gym: gymnasium
Viz: videlicet	Extra: extraordinary
Decal: decalcomania	Telly: television
Plane: airplane, aeroplane	Memo: memorandum
Ere: before	Ken: knowledge
Roach: cockroach	Vac: vacuum cleaner
Cello: violoncello	Chute: parachute

Wig: periwig	Cute: acute
Van: caravan	Van: vanguard
Nylons: nylon stockings	Prefab: prefabricated
Prep: preparatory school	Ref: referee
Hi-fi: high fidelity	Hi-tec: high technology
Intercom:intercommunicator	Sub: subway
Pub: public house	Ed: education, editor
Confab: confabulate	Bio: biography
Pros: professionals	Bike: bicycle
Non-coms:non-commisioned	Oft: often
Copter: helicopter	Mob: mobile
Prom: promenadeconcert	Ult: ultimate
Rep: reputation	Hippo: hippopotamus
Non-sched: non-scheduled	Scope: telescope
Fridge: refrigerator	Dub: double
Exam: examination	Fancy: fantasy
Miss: mistress	Coke: coca-cola
Vegs: vegetables	Fab: fabulous
Cabbie: cabman	Nightie: nightdress

Co-ed: co-educational student

Undergrad: undergraduate

Demov: demobilized

Specs: spectacles

Finals: final examinations

Co-op: cooperative store or society

Maxi: maxi-skirt

Xmas: Christmas

Bib: bibliography

Zoo: zoological park

Gent: gentleman

Logo: Logotype

Perk: percolator

Congrats: congratulations

Psycho: Psychopat

Sci-fi: science fiction

Condo: Condominium

Limo: limousine

Show biz: show business

Prof: professor

Sarge: sergeant

Op: operator

Pop: popular music

Prelims: preliminary examinations

Mini: mini-skirt

Caf: cafeteria

Id: identification

Folk: folklore

Bros: brothers

Toons: cartoons

Champ: champion

Homo: homosexual

Nuke: nuclear

Perv: Perverted

Tux: Tuxedo

Temp: temporary

Rehab: rehabilitation

Detox: Detoxify

Decaf: Decaffeined

Mart: market

Show biz: Show business

Fugee: Refugee

Sec: second

Gas -gasoline

Cuke-cucumber

Squad: squadron

Celeb: celebrity

Dec: detective

Gator: Alligator

Perv: perverted

Thru -through

Info -information

Recap-recapitulation

Fed: federal

Sit-com: Situation comedy

Blendings

Blendings are words produced by combining other words or parts of words in an unusual way.

Some examples of blendings are:

NABISCO: NATIONAL+BISCUIT+COMPANY

QUERY: QUESTION+INQUIRY

BRUNCH: BREAKFAST+LUNCH

SKORT: SKIRT+SHORT

SMOG: SMOKE+FOG

CAMCORDER: CAMERA+RECORDER

MOTEL: MOTORISTS+HOTEL

FRIENDSHIPMENT: FRIENDSHIP+SHIPMENT

SQUIGGLE: SQUIRM+WRIGGLE

SUBURB: SUB+URBAN

SICKLEMIA: SICKLE+CELL+ANAEMIA

SPANGLISH: SPANISH+ENGLISH

FORTNIGHT: FOURTEEN+NIGHTS

MUPPET: MARIONETTE+PUPPET

TRANSIEVER: TRANSMITTER+RECEIVER

SEAFARI: SEA + SAFARI

HUSTING: HUS + THING

HASSLE: HAGGLE + TUSSLE

Chapter 8
Prepositions

One of the most difficult aspects of any language is the correct use of the prepositions. In English not always we find a similar use as in Spanish.

Some of the most frequently misused propositions are:

To aim at

To think of, about

To dream of, about

To smell of

To taste of

To listen to

To wait   a) on (a restaurant)
               b) for (a person)

To agree   a) to (something)
               b) with (someone)

To ask   a) for (pedir)
               b) about (preguntar)
               c) to (invitar)

To compare something or somebody
               a) to (different things)
               b) with (similar things)

It depends on

It consists of

Identical with

Similar to

Slave to

Equal to

The same as

Different from

Bored with or by

To be operated on for something

To be attended to   a) (by a doctor)
                              b) (in a hospital)

To prefer something to something

The key to the door

To be critical of someone or something

To speak on the phone or by phone

Associated with

To shop for

To congratulate someone on something

To account for

To change for

To make a tour of a place

In relation to; related to

In regard to

Regardless of

Linked to

Native to

Indigenous to

Allergic to

Born to (a humble family)

Heir to

Substitute A for B. (You used to have A and now have B)

A need for

In need of

Word by word (una por una)

Word for word (repetir exactamente)

According to

In accord(ance) with

To open the book to a page

To name after (in honor of)

To take pride in

To be proud of

To connect this to that

To count with the fingers on one hand

To be envious, crazy, wild over someone

To be angry, mad at someone

To be obliged, indebted, beholden to someone

Arrive at - or - in

To open the book to page

To preside over

In honor of

Pleased with

Satisfied with

Fill with

On the beach

But: In Varadero beach

On a farm

To play on a team

But to play in a game

To swear on someone

Insult you to your face

To be overprotective of a child

To match something (to/with) something

Disappointed in

To congratulate someone on something

Result in

Combination to a safe

To count to one hundred

To wish upon (a star)

To apply for

Exception to the rule

To live on (someone/something)

To conceive of something

To fill a glass with water

Respectful of

Considerate of

Embark on

Concerned with

Based on (se basa en)

Based in (living, settled)

Based at (a small place)

A synonym for

Synonymous with

Comprised of

On the street (sidewalk)

In the street (pavement)

Attracted to

Embark on

Comprised of

Good luck on something

On my responsibility

On one condition

Tolerant of

Directed at

Chapter 9
Nominal Verbs

The so-called Nominal or Nounal Verbs are very frequently found in English. It is not unusual to see cases of nouns turned into verbs in a very peculiar way.

We have selected a few examples of some of these nounal verbs:

To fan: incentivar, motivar, avivar
  Ex. He carried out his studies fanned by this mother.

To tree: perseguir hasta hacer subir a un árbol
  Ex. The dog treed the cat.

To doctor: aguar, licuar, adulterar
  Ex. They gave the baby doctored milk.
      This bucket contains doctored paint.

To fire: expulsar, botar (del trabajo)
  Ex. He was fired from his work.

To husband: ahorrar
  Ex. You should husband some money for the holidays.

To thumb: pedir una botella (un aventón, auto-stop) en la carretera con el dedo pulgar
  Ex. We thumbed on our way home.

To man: tripular, conducir, manejar
  Ex. The captain manned the ship a long distance.

To bus: limpiar (la mesa)
  Ex. Please, Bessie, bus the table when you finish eating.

To pigeonhole: encasillar
Ex. They have pigeonholed her as a singer though she's an
    all-round actress.

To book: reservar (una entrada, un asiento, etc.)
Ex. We booked a seat for the theater.

To clock: cronometrar
Ex. Juantorena clocked a new record.

To fence: acorralar
Ex. Don't fence me in.

To pen: encerrar, confinar
Ex. The dog was penned in the house.

To people: poblar
Ex. The island was peopled by half-breed.

To fork: bifurcarse
Ex. The causeway forks here.

To rendezvous: encontrarse, reunirse
Ex. We rendezvoused in the gazebo.

To shelve: engavetar
Ex. My record was shelved for years.

To gun: ametrallar
Ex. The murderer was gunned down.

To egg: incitar
Ex. She egged me on to do it.

To pencil: escribir a lápiz
Ex. I penciled her a note.

To shanghai: forzar, obligar
   Ex. He shanghaied her to go with him.

To tailor: adecuar
   Ex. We should tailor the tests.

To face: afrontar, enfrentar
   Ex. You should face the music now.

To stomach: tolerar, soportar
   Ex. I can't stomach her.

To taxi: Viajar en taxi.
   Ex. We taxied to the station.

To mind: ocuparse de, velar por
   Ex. The parents paid a person to mind the children.

To party: fiestar, estar de fiesta
   Ex. Partying is carried out with live and recorded music.

To rock: estremecerse
   Ex. Chile has been rocked several times lately.

To sport: lucir, ostentar
   Ex. She likes to sport her new dress.

To dog-ear: marcar la esquina superior de una página de un libro.
   Ex. The book was dog-eared on page 23.

To cow: acobardarse
   Ex. He cowed when he spoke to her.

To stocking: ponerse o usar medias (de mujer)
   Ex. She had stockinged feet.

To house: albergar
  Ex. The hotel houses 250 people.

To gas: asfixiar
  Ex. He gassed himself.

Sometimes, other classes of words are used as verbs. This is the case of some prepositions, adverbs, conjunctions, adjectives, initials, etcetera.

Prepositions
You find a constant toing and froing during the rush hour.
(gerund)

The credit was upped to 30 pesos.
(verb)

Adverbs
Stop yessing him, please.
(verb)

Conjunctions
He likes to while away.
(verb)

Adjectives
We were briefed about the new plans and programs.
(verb)

Initials
They DDTed the garden.
(verb)

The boxer kayoed the rival (K.O.) (knocked out)
(verb)

She's emceeing (M.C.)
(verb)

We're posslquing here. (POSSLQ) (verb)

113

Interjections
Stop ohing her!
(verb)

Conjunctions
She's always iffing
(verb)

Chapter 10
Word Order In English

Syntax in English is most important, for the order of the words can express a different meaning according to the position they have in an utterance. Such is the situation of the following cases:

Long before: mucho antes

Before Long: en breve

Offspring: prole, descendencia

Spring off: saltar

Layout: diseño.

OutLay: gastos, desembolso.

Look out: mirador

Outlook: perspectiva

Box office: taquilla (de cine)

Office box: apartado postal

Brand new: nuevo de paquete

New brand: nueva marca

A day off: día libre

An off day: día aciago

With colors flying: con banderas al viento

With flying colors: exitosamente

Outcome: resultado

Come out: salir

Output: rendimiento.

Put out: apagar (un incendio)

Input: entrada (de un equipo)

Put in: poner dentro

Outset: comienzo, principio

Set out: partir, salir

Offset: compensar

Set off: separar, dividir

Upset: malhumorado, contrariado

Set up: establecer

Outlet: salida

Let out: dejar escapar

Turn someone on: excitar (sexualmente)

Turn on someone: rebelarse, revirarse

Chapter 11
The Order of Adjectives in English

In English, the adjective precedes the noun, but in case of several adjectives, which one should be placed first?

In this case the order should be:

1	2	3	4	5	6	7	8
Ordinal number	Cardinal number	General	Age	Color	Material	Origin	Noun
		Opinion Size					
		Shape Cost Condition					

Thus:

A shirt, cotton, white: A white cotton shirt.

A handbag; leather, grey: A grey leather handbag.

A sandwich; small, cheese: A small cheese sandwich.

A car; blue, old: An old blue car.

An object; brown, large, metal: A large brown metal object.

A table; red, wooden, old: An old red wooden table.

A house; white, brick, big, new: A big new white brick house.

However, some expressions take the adjective after and not before the noun. These are set expressions mostly from French.

Some examples are the following:

Air conditioned
Pound sterling
The color purple
News brief
Paradise lost
Paradise regained
Secretary General (for International Institutions)
President elect
Meridian zero
Notary public
Court martial
Sum total
Captain General
Attorney General
Governor General
Postmaster general
Cartoon minutes
Foam rubber
Flowers galore (Irish)
Time immemorial
Conduct unbecoming
Heir apparent
Proof positive
Knight errant
The poet laureate
By all means possible
All the people present
Letters patent
Soldier blue
Mother Superior
Professor Emeritus
Code Red

Code Blue
Artist manqué
Child prodigy
Infant prodigy
Knight templar
Vena Cava
Case closed
Prince Charming
Prince Regent
Body Politic
Mission Accomplished
For reasons unknown

Chapter 12
Acronyms

Because of the ever closer connection between the oral and the written forms of the language it is sometimes difficult to differentiate clippings originating in oral speech from graphical abbreviations.These often pass into oral speech and become widely used in conversation.

During World War I and later it became popular, not only in English-speaking countries, but also in other parts of the world to call countries, government agencies and other organizations by the initial abbreviations derived from writing as the USSR the UN, etcetera.

Such words formed from the initials of each major part of a coumpound term are called acronyms.

Two possible types of correlation should be noted between written and spoken forms.

1. If the abbreviation can be read as an ordinary English word, it will be read like one.

Some examples are:

NABISCO - National Biscuit Company

UNESCO - United Nations, Educational, Scientific and Cultural Organization

UNRRA - United Nations Relief and Rehabilitation Administration

Laser - light amplification and stimulated emission radiation

Maser - microwave amplification and stimulated emission radiation

Radar - radio detection and ranging

Jato - jet-assisted takeoff

AIDS - Acquired immune deficiency syndrome

DINK - Dual income, no kids

AWOL - Absent without official leave

G.P. - General purpose

C.B. - Citizens'band

I.V. - Intra venous

YUPPY - Young urban professional

UFO - Unidentified flying object

SWAK - Sealed with a kiss

POSSLQ - Person of opposite sex sharing living quarters

WHO - World Health Organization

CMEA - Council for Mutual and Economic Assistance

UNICEF - United Nations International Children's Emergency Fund

SEATO - South East Asia Treaty Organization

NATO - North Atlantic Treaty Organization

NASA - National Aeronautics and Space Administration

UFTAA - Universal Federation of Travel Agents Association

TGIF - Thanks God it's Friday!

IOU - I owe you

G.P.A. - General Performance Average

D.T. - Delirium Tremens

A.T.V. - All terrain vehicle

K.P. - Kitchen Police

FAX - Fax Access Xerocopy

DHL -   Dalsei Adrian
        Hillblom Larry
        Lynn Robert

2. The other subgroup consists of initial abbreviations with alphabetic reading retained.

Some examples are:

QT - on the quiet; in secret

R.S.V.P. - repondez, s'il vous plait

I.Q. - Intelligence quotient

M.C. - Master of Ceremony

U.T.C. Universal time coordinates

E.T. - Extraterrestrial

U.S.S.R. - Union of Soviet Socialist Republics

F.R.G. - Federal Republic of Germany

G.D.R. - German Democratic Republic

P.A. system - Public address system

P.T.A. - Parent teacher association

B.B.C. - British Broadcasting Corporation

G.I. - Government Issue

M.P. - Member of Parliament

U.S.A - United States of America

C.W.T. - a hundred weight (quintal en el sistema de unidades de masa de Gran Bretaña)

P.M. - Prime Minister

Y.C.L. - Young Communist League

V.I.P. - Very Important Person

S.O.S. - Save our Souls (radio code signal of extreme distress)

P.O.W. - Prisoner of war

K.O. - Knocked out

P.T.O - Please, turn over

W.C. - Water closet

C.I.F. - Cost of insurance and freight

F.O.B. - Free on board

S.O.B. - Son of a bitch

G.P. - General purpose

U.T.C. - Universal Time Coordinates

P.T. - Physical Training

A.S.A.P. - As soon as possible

A.D.I.D.A.S. - All day I dream about sports

T.I.P. - To insure promptness

I.C.U. - Intensive care unit

Chapter 13
American English and British English:
Any Difference?

English on both sides of the Atlantic

The following sign once appeared, it is said, in a Paris shop window:

"English spoken-American understood"

The French aren't the only ones who have made humorous references to the differences between these two "languages". Oscar Wilde, the Irish dramatist, commented:

"The English have really everything in common with the Americans, except of course language".

An English literary critic spoke of being "bilingual in the two branches of English", and Russell Baker once began one of his columns in the New York Times this way: "One of the hardest languages for an American to learn is English". He was referring to British English.

Is the English spoken in the United States a different language from the English spoken in Great Britain?

H.L. Mencken, an American who shortly after World War I published his book *The American Language*, evidently thought so. But no serious modern linguist holds this opinion. The grammatical structure is for the most part the same. There are, of course, many differences in pronunciation and some in spelling. The British write colour; Americans write color. The British write theatre; Americans write theater.

And there are quite a number of differences in vocabulary as well. Norman W. Schur, in *British Self-taught With Comments in American*, points out that an Englishwoman looking in a store window would probably say: "I'd like to go into that shop and look at that frock", while her friend from the United (States would more likely say, "I'd like to go into that store and look at that dress".The Englishwoman might have said "shop", but would never have said "frock". And the person who waited on them would be a "salesperson" in the United States, but a "shop assistant" in England.

No one would argue with the fact that there are many differences between British English and American English. But the similarities between them are far greater than the differences. And with modern communications-the British watching telly and going to the cinema on one side of the Atlantic and Americans watching TV and going to the movies on the other-these two dialects of English are moving closer together all the time.

British English

The main dialectal variants of British English are Northern, Midland, Eastern, Western, Southern, Scottish and Irish. Every group contains several dialects.

The Scottish and the Irish variants have special importance because of the literature composed in them. Robert Burns, the great national poet of Scotland, is known all over the world. Today there is a whole new group of poets writing in this variant of the English language.

One of the best known dialects of the Southern group is Cockney, the regional dialect of London. As spoken by the educated lower middle classes, it is marked by some deviations in pronunciation, but few in vocabulary, morphology and syntax. As spoken by the uneducated, however, Cockney differs from Standard English not only in pronunciation but also in vocabulary, morphology and syntax.

American English

The variety of English spoken in the United States has received the name of American English.

Naturally, the American language is not monolithic, but consists of numerous dialects; their literary normalized form is called Standard American.

The regional dialect areas in the United States are larger than those of Britain.

The three major dialect regions are the Northern, the Midland, and the Southern; the Midland region is divided into North Midland and South Midland. Each dialect region in turn can be subdivided into subdialect areas whose exact number is as yet uncertain.

The major differences between the standard forms of British and American English become readily apparent upon observation. There are noticeable differences in pronunciation, especially of the vowels as in words like home, hot, aunt.

Grammatical differences also exist, for an American would say: do you have the time? while an Englishman would say: have you got the time?

The chief differences, however, occur in vocabulary. The historical causes of these deviations can be traced back to the language spoken by the first settlers in the new continent, that is, to the English of the seventeenth century. For more than three centuries, the American vocabulary developed more or less independently and was influenced by the surroundings.

The early Americans had to coin words for the unfamiliar flora, fauna, and names for such topographical features as creek, swamp, etcetera.

The opposition between the variants belonging to the lexical systems of British and American English is of great linguistic value, because it furnishes ample data for observing the influence of extra-linguistic factors upon the vocabulary.

Regarding vocabulary some common examples are the following:

American English	British English
Window shade	Blind
Crepe	Pancake
Bureau	Chest of drawers
Dial tone	Dialling tone
Tail pipe	Exhaust pipe
Earthenware	Crockery
Floor lamp	Standing lamp
Silverware	Cutlery
Gas pedal	Accelerator
Clipping	Cutting
Raincoat	Waterproof, Mackintosh
Saline solution	Drips
Apartment	Flat
Bathrobe	Dressing gown

Vacation	Holiday
Streetcar	Tram
Policeman, cop	Bobby, cop
Truck	Lorry
Elevator	Lift
Baggage	Luggage
Freight car	Goods wagon
Conductor	Guard
Driver	Motorist
Trailer	Caravan
Windshield	Windscreen
Vest	Waistcoat
Pants	Trousers
Mail	Post
Fender	Bumper
Licence plate	Number plate
Hood	Bonnet
Trunk	Boot
Mailman	Postman

Faucet	Tap
Movies	Cinema
Package	Parcel
Can	Tin
Dumb	Stupid, thick
Gas	Petrol
Line	Queue
Drug store	Chemist's
Stewardess	Air hostess
Cookies	Biscuits
Baby buggy or carriage	Pram
Garbage can	Dustbin
The line is busy	The line is engaged
Argument	Row, argument
A flat tire	A puncture
T.V.	Telly, T.V.
Expensive	Dear
Rent a car	Hire a car
Dress	Frock

Suspenders	Braces
To phone	To give a ring, to phone
Salesman	Shop assistant
Railroad	Railway
Sidewalk	Footway, pavement
Sideburns	Sideboards
Fire department	Fire brigade
Grade crossing	Level crossing
Furnace	Boiler
Billboard	Boarding
Cowcatcher	Plough
Candy	Sweets
Mailbox	Letter-box
Rooster	Cock
Dollar bill	Pound note
Plate	Dish
Tag	Label
Scotch tape	Sellotape
Free time	Spare time

Parking lot	Car park
Price	Fare
One-way ticket	Single ticket
Bookstore	Bookshop
Cab	Taxi
Stretcher	Couch
Monkey wrench	Spanner
Street musician	Busker
Band-aid	Elastoplast
Subway	Underground
Fall	Autumn
Cooker	Stove
Refrigerator	Fridge
Liquor store	Off-license
Pacifier	Dummy
Restroom	Public convenience
Eraser	Rubber
Janitor	Caretaker
Floor	Ground, level

To fire (a person)	To sack (a person)
Antenna	Aerial
Closet	Wardrobe
Diaper	Nappy
Drapes	Curtain
Freeway	Motorway
Kerosene	Paraffin
Thief	Burglar
Smokestack	Chimney
Flashlight	Torch
Yard	Garden
Wire	Telegram
Sucker	Lollipop
Bureau	Chest of drawers
Streetlight	Lamppost
Mortician	Undertaker
What brand is it?	What make is it?
Go to the toilet	Go to the loo
Overpass	Flyover

Concerning spelling, there are some differences between British English and American English.

American English	British English
Offense	Offence
Practice	Practise
Airplane	Aeroplane
Traveler	Traveller
Jeweler	Jeweller
Counselor	Counsellor
Center, theater	Centre, theatre
Color, favor, humor	Colour, favour, humour
Organization	Organisation
Connection	Connexion
Program	Programme
Jail	Gaol
Pajamas	Pyjamas
Curb	Kerb
Check	Cheque
Plow	Plough

Story	Storey
Tire	Tyre
Cozy	Cosy
Apologize	Apologise
Gray	Grey
Aluminum	Aluminium
Wagon	Waggon
Judgment	Judgement
Leukosis	Leucosis
Sulfate	Sulphate
Diarrhea	Diarrhoea
Esophagus	Oesophagus
Anemia	Anaemia
Anesthesia	Anaesthesia
Cecum	Caecum
Cecal	Caecal
Feces	Faeces
Hem	Haem
Hematology	Haematology

Hemorrhage	Haemorrhage
Criticize	Criticise
Realize	Realise
Utilize	Utilise
Realization	Realisation
Utilization	Utilisation
Labeled	Labelled
Labeling	Labelling
Traveler	Traveller
Anestrum	Anoestrum
Estrus	Oestrus
Dyspneal	Dyspnoeal
Pyorrhea	Pyorrhoea
Mold	Mould
Molt	Moult
Behavior	Behaviour
Labor	Labour
Fiber	Fibre
Titer	Titre

Aluminum	Aluminium
Check	Cheque
Gram	Gramme
Judgment	Judgement
Leukocyte	Leucocyte
Leukosis	Leucosis
License	Licence
Sulfate	Sulphate
Wagon	Waggon

In regard to pronunciation, some examples could be the following:

Tomato

Either, neither

Vase

Lavatory, secretary, laboratory

Behind

And all the endings "er" as in father, mother, brother, sister, never, ever, forever, spare, etcetera.
Some verbs are different in their past forms in British and American.

American	British
bet-bet-bet	bet-betted-betted
burned	burnt
dreamed	dreamt
dwelled	dwelt
leaned	leant
learned	learnt
smelled	smelt
spelled	spelt
spilled	spilt
spoiled	spoilt

Chapter 14
Poetry

Shift of Meaning

A large amount of words formerly had a different meaning from the one they convey today. The reader of modern English often fails to recognize that a word has changed the meaning it had long ago, let alone the meaning of today. The following piece of poetry is a sample of that shift of meaning.

GROOVY, MAN, GROOVY

Remember when Hippy meant big in the hips,
and a trip involved travel in cars, planes and ships?
When pot was a vessel for cooking things in,
and hooked was what Grandmother's rug might have been?
When fix was a verb that meant mend or repair,
and be-in meant merely existing somewhere?
When neat meant well organized, tidy and clean,
and grass was a ground cover, normally green?
When lights and not people were switched on and off,
and the pill might have been what you took for a cough?
When camp meant to quarter outdoors in a tent,
and pop was where the weasel went?
When groovy meant furrowed with channels and hollows,
and birds were wing'd creatures like robins and swallows?
When fuzz was substance, real fluffy like lint,
and bread came from bakeries not from the mint?
When square meant a 90-degree angled form,
and cool was a temperature not quite warm?
When roll meant a bun, and rock was a stone,
and hang up was something you did with a phone?
When chicken meant poultry and bag meant a sack,
with junk trashy cast offs and old bric a brac?
When Jam was preserves that you spread on your bread,
and crazy meant balmy, not right in the head?
When cat was a feline, a cat grown up,
and the tea was a liquid you drank from a cup?

When swinger was someone who swang on a swing,
and pad was a soft sort of cushiony thing?
When way out meant distant and far, far away,
and a man couldn't sue you for calling him gay?
When tough described meat too unyielding to chew,
uand making a scene was a rude thing to do?
Words once so sensible, sober and serious,
are making the freak scene, like psychodelirious.
It's groovy, man, groovy, but English it's not.
Methinks that our language is going to pot.

English is Tough Stuff

Dearest creature in creation
Study English pronunciation
I will teach you in my verse
Sounds like corpse, corps, horse and worse.
I will keep you, Suzy, busy
Make your head with heat grow dizzy.
Tear in eye you dress will tear.
So shall I! Oh hear my prayer.
Just compare heart, beard, and heard,
Dies and diet, lord and word,
Sword and sward, retain and Britain.
(Mind the latter, how it's written.)
Now I surely will not plague you
With such words as plaque and argue.
But be careful how you speak:
Say break and steak, but bleak and streak;
Cloven, oven, how and low,
Script, receipt, show, poem and toe.
Hear me say, devoid of trickery,
Daughter, laughter, and Terpsichore,
Typhoid, measles, topsails, aisles,
Exiles, similes, and reviles;
Scholar, vicar, and cigar,
Solar, mica, war and far;
One, anemone, Balmoral,
Kitchen, lichen, laundry, laurel;
Gertrude, German, wind and mind,
Scene, Melpomene, mankind.
Billet does not rhyme with ballet,
Bouquet, wallet, mallet, chalet.
Blood and flood are not like food,
Nor is mould like should or would.
Viscous, viscount, loaf and broad,
Toward, to forward, to reward.
And your pronunciation's OK
When you correctly say croquet,

Rounded, wounded, grieve and sieve,
Friend and fiend, alive and live.
Ivy, privy, famous; clamour
And enamour rhyme with hammer.
River, rival, tomb, bomb, comb,
Doll and roll and some and home.
Stranger does not rhyme with anger,
Neither does devour with clangour.
Souls but foul, haunt but aunt,
Font, front, wont, want, grand, and grant,
Shoes, goes, does. Now first say finger,
and then singer, ginger, linger,
Real, zeal, mauve, gauze, gouge and gauge,
Marriage, foliage, mirage, and age.
Query does not rhyme with very,
Nor does fury sound like bury.
Dost, lost, post and doth, cloth, loth.
Job, nob, bosom, transom, oath.
Though the differences seem very little,
We say actual but victual.
Refer does not rhyme with deafer.
Foeffer does, and zephyr, heifer.
Mint, pint, senate and sedate;
Dull, bull, and George ate late.
Scenic, Arabic, Pacific,
Science, conscience, scientific.
Liberty, library, heavy and heaven,
Rachel, ache, moustache, eleven.
We say hallowed, but allowed,
People, leopard, towed, but vowed.
Mark the differences, moreover,
Between mover, cover, clover;
Leeches, breeches, wise, precise,
Chalice, but police and lice;
Camel, constable, unstable,
Principle, disciple, label.
Petal, panel, and canal,
Wait, surprise, plait, promise, pal.

Worm and storm, chaise, chaos, chair,
Senator, spectator, mayor.
Tour, but our and succour, four.
Gas, alas, and Arkansas.
Sea, idea, Korea, area,
Psalm, Maria, but malaria.
Youth, south, southern, cleanse and clean.
Doctrine, turpentine, marine.
Face, but preface, not efface.
Phlegm, phlegmatic, ass, glass, bass.
Large, but target, gin, give, verging,
Ought, out, joust and scour, scourging.
Ear, but earn and wear and tear
Does not rhyme with here but ere.
Hyphen, roughen, nephew Stephen,
Monkey, donkey, Turk and jerk,
Ask, grasp, wasp, and cork and work.
Pronunciation, think oh Psyche!
Is a paling stout and spikey?
Won't it make you loose your wits,
Writing groats and saying grits?
It's a dark abyss or tunnel:
Strewn with stones, stowed, solace, gunwale,
Islington and Isle of Wright,
Housewife, verdict and indict.
Finally, which rhymes with enough
Though, through, plough, or dough, or cough?
Hiccough has the sound of cup.
My advice is to give up!!

Bibliography

Abrams, Sharon and Rein, David P. *Spectrum 4: A Communicative Course in English*. New York: Regents Publishing Co. Inc. New York, N.Y.1981.

Alexander L.G. (1974) *Practice and Progress (New Concept English)*. La Habana, Cuba: Editorial Pueblo y Educación.

Baugh, Albert C. (1935) *History of the English Language*. New York: Appleton-Century Crofts, Inc.

Copley, J. (1964) Shift of Meaning. London: Oxford University.

Guilland Daphne M. and Hinds-Howell David G. (1986) *Dictionary of English Idioms*. Middlesex, England: Penguin Books Ltd.

Harvey Paul and Walker Carolyn (1986) *Way Ahead, Coursebook 3*. England: Penguin Books.

Institutos Superiores Pedagógicos (1982) *A Course in English Lexicology*. La Habana, Cuba: Editorial Pueblo y Educación.

Kenyon, John Samuel and Knott, Thomas Albert (1972) *A Pronouncing Dictionary of American English*. La Habana, Cuba: Instituto Cubano del Libro.

McArthur, Tom (1986) *Longman Lexicon of Contemporary English*. England: Longman Group Limited, Volumes 1 and 2, La Habana, Cuba: Edición Revolucionaria.

Thorndike, E.L. (1941) Thorndike Dictionary New York: Scott, Foresman and Company.

Watcyn-Jones, Peter (1985) Test Your Vocabulary, Volumes 1, 2, 3 and 4. Great Britain: Penguin Books.

Witherspoon, Alexander M. (1943) *Common Errors in English and How to Avoid Them*. New York: Permabooks

About the Author

Jesús Núñez Romay is a Professor of English at the University of Havana, Cuba. He is an Associate Professor at the National Center for Scientific Research, University of Havana, Cuba and has 35 years of experience in Higher Education.

He is the author of *Post-Revolutionary Cuban Spanish: A Glossary of Social, Political, and Common Terms (Spanish – English) [Glosario de términos socio-políticos y autóctones de actualidad (español-inglés)]*.

Ordering blue ocean press books:

Individual orders:
> Books can be purchased and ordered from your local bookstore.
>
> Books can also be purchased online through retailers such as: the Amazon sites (com, co.uk, co.jp, fr, ca, de) Barnes and Nobles (bn.com), Powells.com, Abebooks.com, Alibris.com, etc.

Institutional Buyers, Booksellers, and Libraries:
> Books can be ordered from the following distributors and wholesalers:

U.S. and Canada
Ingram Book Group (ipage/Ingram, Ingram Library Services, Ingram International)
Baker & Taylor
NACSCORP (a wholly-owned, for-profit subsidiary of the National Association of College Stores)

U.K. and Rest of the World
Gardners Books
Bertrams
Baker & Taylor
Ingram International

www.ingramcontent.com/pod-product-compliance
Lightning Source LLC
Chambersburg PA
CBHW031127020426
42333CB00012B/263